~~10.00~~
12.00
5.00
___
17.0

GNOSTICISM AND
EARLY CHRISTIANITY

About the author:

Dr. Grant is Professor in the Divinity School
and the Federated Theological Faculty of
the University of Chicago, and an ordained
minister of the Episcopal Church. His interest in Gnosticism began in Holland where
he spent a year as a Fulbright Research
Professor and a Guggenheim fellow.

GNOSTICISM

AND EARLY

CHRISTIANITY

BY R. M. GRANT

Second Edition

COLUMBIA UNIVERSITY PRESS 1966

NEW YORK & LONDON

To Douglas, Peter, Susan, and Jimmy

PREFACE

THIS BOOK consists of six lectures prepared and delivered under the auspices of the Committee on the History of Religions of the American Council of Learned Societies.* They were given, either as a whole or in part, during the academic year 1957–1958, at the University of Pennsylvania, Princeton University, Columbia University, Union Theological Seminary, Harvard Divinity School, Brown University, the University of Toronto, Yale University, Emory University, Agnes Scott College, Columbia Theological Seminary, the University of Georgia, and Northwestern University (with Garrett Biblical Institute and Seabury-Western Theological Seminary). It need hardly be said that the author, a student of the New Testament and early Church history, did not venture to cross the minefield of Gnosticism without an escort. Before, during, and after the lectures he received the invaluable counsel and criticism of many scholars; among them were Henry Chadwick, Erwin R. Goodenough, F. C. Grant, Moshe Greenberg, Hans Jonas, the lamented Ralph Marcus, A. D. Nock, Gilles Quispel, G. Scholem, and Krister Stendahl. None of them, of course, is in any way responsible

* A new essay, "Beyond Judaism and Christianity," has been added for the second edition.

for what the author has finally said. But all of them, and others as well, contributed to the pressure which induced him to rewrite most of the lectures.

The basic theory here set forth is not new, as references along the way will make plain. The only novelty is perhaps the attempt to explain Gnosticism as arising out of the debris of apocalyptic-eschatological hopes which resulted from the fall or falls of Jerusalem. It must be admitted that other disappointments are found in the first century of our era; the followers of the "false prophets" described by Josephus must have suffered in this way. But the most crushing blow of all must have come when God failed to save his city of Jerusalem. Only after this disaster do we encounter Gnosticism in its various systematic forms. The fallacy in the author's argument may be his identification of *post hoc* with *propter hoc*. We shall see.

The translations from Greek and Latin documents are those of the author unless they are explicitly ascribed to someone else; for Coptic and Syriac writings he has used English, French, or German translations. Translations from the Bible will often differ from ordinary versions because of the author's attempt to render passages in a somewhat "Gnostic" way.

R. M. G.

Federated Theological Faculty
University of Chicago
January, 1959

CONTENTS

1

THE NATURE OF GNOSTICISM

IT IS sometimes difficult to tell why various objects of scholarly concern arouse interest, not only in academic circles but also outside them. We can be sure, however, that in universities, as elsewhere, new occasions teach new duties, and that fresh archaeological discoveries are likely to arouse enthusiasm. The Dead Sea Scrolls provide conspicuous examples. Students of the Bible had long been aware of the importance of the Jewish apocalypses produced during the period when Christianity arose, but the discovery of the Qumran library reinforced their awareness and added a great many new materials, the significance of which has still not been fully assessed.[1] Similar discoveries made in Egypt at about the same time have brought many scholars to focus their attention on Gnosticism and have provided further support for the position of those who regard it as important for the interpretation of early Christian documents. Indeed, it now looks as if the data derived both from Qumran and from Nag-Hammadi will require a fairly complete rewriting of early Christian history, since in large measure this history is the history of the relation of the early Church to its environment. Since in some way the

Essenes of Qumran seem to be related to the later development of Jewish Christianity, it is obvious that a fresh interpretation of the data previously known will have to be made.

In the course of this work of reinterpretation, older testimonies may be neglected in favor of what is new. It may be that the Hellenistic and Greco-Roman elements in Judaism and in early Christianity will be temporarily overshadowed by the exciting sectarian and apocalyptic motifs just discovered or rediscovered. To some extent our discussion will fail to escape this error, and we must certainly admit at the outset that more could be said about Greek elements in Gnosticism than will be said here. It seems fairly plain, however, that in the past the Jewish element, or rather the very heterodox Jewish element, in Gnostic thought has been neglected, and it deserves presentation even in a somewhat one-sided way. "There must be divisions of opinion among you, so that those people"—or rather, those opinions—"which are approved may become evident among you" (1 Cor. 11.19).

In the course of our discussion we shall first treat the sources of our information about Gnosticism; next we shall try to provide some sort of definition of its salient features, at least; then we shall try to show that it originated in a crisis in Jewish apocalyptic thought during the first two centuries of our era (Chapter 1). In Chapter 2 we shall attempt to set forth some of the ways in which the Gnostic picture of the heavenly world emerged out of considerations originally calendrical in nature and related to emphases characteristic of Jewish apocalyptic, though in dealing with the Ophites we shall have to go well beyond Judaism; and we shall discuss the way in which Yahweh came to be regarded as hostile to mankind, and the possible origins of the Gnostic doctrine of a redeemer descended from heaven. In Chapter 3 we shall endeavor to disentangle the threefold strand of traditions related to Simon Magus, often regarded by the Church Fathers as the founder of Gnosticism, and shall then briefly discuss other systems whose attitudes toward the Jewish law were like those of the Simonians. At this point we shall turn to the Syrian Gnosis specifically related to Christian ideas of salvation, examining the systems of Saturninus and the Apocryphon of John and tracing some of their sources (Chapter 4). In Chapter 5 we shall consider the major Gnostic systems of the second century, those of Marcion, Valentinus, and Basilides, along with a cursory glance at more philosophical, less Gnostic teachings. Finally, in Chapter 6, we shall turn back to the development of early Christian thought and shall try to discover what influence, if any, Gnostic ideas exercised on various early Christian teachers.

SOURCES

It is always appropriate for the historian to begin a discussion by listing the sources of his information. So we begin by simply naming a few of the more important Church Fathers who discussed Gnostic systems: Justin at Rome about 150–165; Irenaeus at Lyons around 180; Hippolytus

at Rome about 230; Epiphanius in Cyprus about 375; and
so on down to Theodore bar Konai in the eighth century.[2]
But how did these Fathers know what they said they
knew? Naturally enough, they copied their predecessors'
works. Irenaeus copied Justin; Hippolytus and Epiphanius
copied Irenaeus. But they added the products of their own
research. Irenaeus knew Valentinians in Gaul, and he got
hold of their works, as well as the Apocryphon of John,
which we shall presently discuss. Hippolytus was asked by
Gnostics to give a more accurate account of their doctrines
than that provided by Irenaeus. Epiphanius tells us that in
his youth some very beautiful Gnostic women almost persuaded him to join their group; but at the last moment he
decided to report them to the police instead. C. W. King
suggested that Epiphanius is not telling the whole truth.[3]
We cannot be certain. In any event, since most of these
patristic writers reproduced Gnostic documents, scholars
actually had materials for reconstructing some of the
systems. Patristic writings are still valuable sources.

   In the last century or so a good many writings of the
Gnostics themselves have turned up, mostly in Coptic
versions. *Pistis Sophia* shed a good deal of light on Gnostic
thought in decline.[4] But the most important find of the
nineteenth century came in 1896, when the Berlin Museum
bought a papyrus codex of the fifth century. It contains
three Gnostic writings: the Gospel of Mary, the Apocryphon of John, and the Sophia of Jesus Christ. In 1907 Carl
Schmidt pointed out that the Apocryphon was certainly the

source used by Irenaeus to describe the system of the Sethian-Ophites.[5] But because of various vicissitudes these Gnostic writings were not published until Walter Till edited them in 1955.[6] Another version of the Apocryphon appeared in 1956.

Meanwhile, in 1945 near Nag-Hammadi in upper Egypt a large jar was found which contained a fifth-century Coptic Gnostic library. It consisted of at least thirteen leather-bound books, with a total of forty-eight Gnostic treatises on more than seven hundred pages.[7] Most of these volumes are in the possession of the Coptic Museum in Cairo, though one made its way to Europe and was bought in 1952 for the Jung Institute in Zurich. This volume contains the famous Gospel of Truth, probably written by the second-century Gnostic Valentinus; it was edited in 1956 by Malinine, Puech, and Quispel.[8] Other volumes, not yet published, contain Gnostic gospels, apocalypses, epistles, secret traditions, dialogues, and theological treatises. Among them are three different versions of the Apocryphon of John. Till was able to use one of these versions in preparing his edition of the Berlin writings.

At the present time only three volumes of the Nag-Hammadi writings have been published, though more are promised for the near future. These are (1) the edition of the Gnostic writings contained in the Berlin Coptic papyrus, in which, as we have said, Till included variant readings from a Nag-Hammadi version of the Apocryphon of John; (2) the Gospel of Truth; and (3) reproductions of

the pages of the first volume, which includes the Discourse
on the Resurrection, the Apocryphon of John, the gospels
of Thomas and Philip, and the Hypostasis of the Archons.[9]
Many additional details about all the writings are provided
not only in a very important article by H. C. Puech [10] but
also in a book recently published by Jean Doresse.[11]

(It should be added that the "Gnostic gems" discussed
by C. W. King in *The Gnostics and Their Remains* are
not—as he realized—Gnostic; but their relation to gnosis
and to magic deserves further study.[12])

DEFINITION

Defining Gnosticism is an extraordinarily difficult task,
since modern writers use the term to cover a wide variety
of speculative religious phenomena. These phenomena are
encountered from Gaul in the West to Iran in the East,
from the first century of our era to at least the ninth. (In
the early years of this century there were Gnostic churches
in Lyons, but they sound like anachronisms.) [13] There are
systems which ambivalently love and scorn the world and
systems which explicitly hate the world. The systems include notions related to Zoroastrianism, Babylonian religion, Judaism, Hellenistic philosophy and religion, and
Christianity. How are we to define Gnosticism as a whole?

The Christian Clement of Alexandria has provided us
with a systematic analysis of the various names given the
Gnostic sects.[14] Some derived their names from their
founders: Valentinians, Marcionites, Basilidians. Others

were named after their place of origin (Peratikoi) or their nationality (Phrygians). In other cases, the names came from their activities (Encratites, "the continent ones"), their doctrines (Docetists, Haimatitoi [otherwise unknown]), the objects of their enthusiasm or worship (Cainites, Ophites [from ὄφις, serpent]), or from their immoral practices (certain Simonians called Entychites, from their promiscuity). It is not clear whether they applied these names to themselves or not. Probably, most of the names were given them by their opponents. In any event, the varieties of names illustrate the variety present among the sects.

Yet there was something about all these systems which has made it possible for writers ancient and modern to treat them together, to call them Gnostic. The very word *gnosis* shows that the Gnostic *knows*. He does not know because he has gradually learned; he knows because revelation has been given him. He does not believe, for faith is inferior to gnosis. And his gnosis, "the knowledge of the ineffable greatness," is itself perfect redemption. Two famous definitions come from the Valentinians.[15] The first explains that "gnosis is redemption of the inner, spiritual man," not of the body or the soul. The second tells what the questions are to which gnosis provides answers. Gnostics know

who we were and what we have become; where we were or where we had been made to fall; whither we are hastening, whence we are being redeemed; what birth is and what rebirth is.

The questions asked here are certainly not Gnostic. We find them asked and answered by two of the Jewish Christian Apostolic Fathers. Clement, for example, says,

Let us consider from what matter we were made, of what sort and who we were when we came into the world, from what tomb and darkness he who formed and made us brought us into his world, and prepared his benefits for us before we were born [1 Clem. 38.3].

And Barnabas shows how a similar formula could be related to prophecy.

It is written how the Father commands him to redeem us from darkness and to prepare a holy people for himself [Isa. 42.6–7]. We know, then, whence we have been redeemed [Barn. 14.6–7].

The implicit Gnostic answers of the Valentinians make the statement Gnostic. For Gnostics know that they were originally spiritual beings who have come to live in souls and bodies; they once dwelt in the spiritual world above but have been made to fall into this world of sense and sin.[16] Now, thanks to their self-knowledge, they are hastening back above, having been redeemed from this world below. We were born into it, but now we are reborn into the spiritual world.

And once we have mentioned self-knowledge, we can go on to say that this is the chief gnosis of all. The Gnostic is a Gnostic because he knows, by revelation, who his true self is. Other religions are in varying measure God-centered. The Gnostic is self-centered. He is concerned with mythological details about the origin of the universe

and of mankind, but only because they express and illuminate his understanding of himself. This point is clearly expressed in the advice given by a certain Monoimus.[17]

Abandon the search for God and the creation and other matters of a similar sort. Look for him by taking *yourself* as the
starting point. Learn who it is who *within you* makes everything his own and says, "*My* god, *my* mind, *my* thought, *my*
soul, *my* body." Learn the sources of sorrow, joy, love, hate.
Learn how it happens that one watches without willing, rests
without willing, becomes angry without willing, loves without
willing. If you carefully investigate these matters you will find
him *in yourself.*

The Gnostic approach to life is thus a "passionate subjectivity" which counts the world well lost for the sake
of self-discovery.

One might suppose that it was only the more philosophical Gnostic systems which interpreted gnosis in this way.
But from our earliest, most mythological sources we find
evidence of the same attitude. The great event in the story
of Simon Magus was his coming to Tyre, where he found
and redeemed a prostitute named Helen, and made her realize that she was the divine Thought through which the
world had been made, that she had been imprisoned by
hostile angels, that now she was free again. In the system
of Saturninus of Antioch, men come to realize that their
essence is a divine spark of life which can return above to
the unknown god. For Basilides, the Ophites, and the
Valentinians, the continuing work of Christ is to rescue
those who are his from the world below. Like the prodigal

son, the gnostic first "comes to himself" (Luke 15.17), and then returns to the father he had forgotten.

This is the first and most important point in defining Gnosticism. It is a religion of saving knowledge, and the knowledge is essentially self-knowledge, recognition of the divine element which constitutes the true self. To this recognition is added a bewildering variety of myths and cultic practices. These myths and cultic practices vary in details because of the different understandings of the self which different Gnostics have. Thus, for some groups the basic problem of the self is caused by conventional morality, what Freudians call the claims of the superego. These groups ordinarily regard redemption as release from convention. They tell a myth of a great Mother who loves them, who, like them, has been imprisoned and mistreated by hostile powers which have laid down the rules of convention in order to enslave them. Other groups regard redemption as release from the world itself, the world of material existence, and they tell a myth of an unknown Father who wants to free their spirit from the world and take them to himself. They practice a rigid asceticism so that their spirit will not be defiled by the material world and its pleasures. And, of course, in some groups there is a combination of both elements which results in an oscillation between unconventional and hyper-conventional behavior, and in an extremely complicated mythology.

Mythology is a significant feature of all Gnostic systems. It is significant first because it represents an attempt by the Gnostic to explain how his situation arose and how he can get out of it. It is significant also because of its very nature.

Here we cannot differentiate the earlier Gnostic systems from the later ones. In later systems there is a tremendous effort to incorporate myths of every kind into the structure of Gnostic thought. The Gnostic Justin tells us that if we know his story we can understand all kinds of mythology.[18] But this amalgamating tendency was present at the very beginnings of Gnosticism. In the system of Simon Magus we probably encounter not only the Jewish Sophia but also the Babylonian Ishtar; we certainly encounter both Helen of Troy and the goddess Athena. But we must not exaggerate the significance of mythology in Gnosticism. We can easily find myth in the sacred literature of its competitors, for example, in the first chapters of Genesis, which stimulated the imaginations of Jews, Christians, and Gnostics alike. (Moreover, in recent times it has become possible to study the development of Valentinianism and to see how speculation gradually came to be "mythologized.")

Kerényi has cited three passages from Irenaeus which, he thinks, show how the love of myth produced Gnostic theology. The passages are well worth quoting.[19]

Let us now look at their unstable opinion—how, when there are two or three of them, they do not say the same things about these matters but express opposite opinions as to contents and names.

Every day each one of them, in so far as he is able, produces some novelty. For no one is "perfect" among them who is not productive of great lies.

Since they disagree with one another in teaching and in tradition, and the more recent converts pretend to find something new every day and to produce what no one ever thought of, it is difficult to describe the opinions of each.

These passages, however, do not show that mythology was characteristic of Gnosticism. They show that Gnostics valued the free play of creative imagination; indeed, we might well be reading a hostile account of proceedings in a rabbinic school devoted to haggadic exposition of the Old Testament. The passages show that Irenaeus liked uniformity, while the Gnostics he was attacking were fond of variety and novelty. The same emphasis on novelty is to be found in the thought of Marcion, with whom mythological ideas played a very small part.

Gnostics were ultimately devoted not to mythology but to freedom. Speculation and mythology were aspects of this freedom, which involved freedom from astral spirits, from the god of the Old Testament, from the tyranny of the creation, from Old Testament law or any law. Hans Jonas has rightly insisted upon this point.[20]

Gnostic self-knowledge, the result of revelation, is salvation; it issues in freedom and a fresh sense of creativity. So we find it described in the Gospel of Truth.[21]

He who knows is a being from above. If he is called, he hears, he replies, he turns to him who calls him, in order to come back to him. And he knows what he is called. Possessing gnosis, he carries out the will of him who has called him; he desires to do what pleases him. He receives rest. He who thus possesses gnosis knows whence he has come and whither he goes. He knows, like a man who has been drunk and awakens from the drunkenness in which he was, returning to himself and restoring what belongs to him.

As Puech expresses it, using psychological terms, "from an 'alienated' existence we return to our ontological condition, to the deep, total and permanent reality of our ego; we pass, as our writings say, from the domain of the 'cosmos,' from the temporal and phenomenal world to the aeon, to the eternal and non-temporal." [22]

But even if this existentialist-psychological meaning is to be found in our texts—and there is a good deal of resemblance between gnosis and existentialism—we must still inquire about the historical ways in which this meaning came to be expressed. After all, a gap of nearly two thousand years separates ancient Antioch, Alexandria, and Rome from modern Heidelberg or St. Germain des Près. We must ask the traditional historical question about origins.

ORIGINS

In modern times there have been four principal explanations of the origins of Gnosticism. [23] In the opinions of various scholars, Gnosticism arose out of (1) Hellenistic philosophy, (2) oriental religion, chiefly Iranian, (3) Christianity, or (4) heterodox Judaism. One cannot deny that elements of all these viewpoints are to be found in Gnosticism, and the problem is made more difficult because of the interrelations among them. It is extraordinarily difficult, if not impossible, to find witnesses for any one of the viewpoints in a pure form, untouched by one or more of the others. The second-century Gnostics whose systems we know were influenced by Christianity, and it is only by inference that we can argue that there is a pre-Christian gnosis. On the other hand, if we leave aside the theological

explanation of Gnosticism as due to demonic activity, the
earliest account we possess of its origin treats it as based on
sectarian Judaism.

This account was provided about the year 170 by the
Jewish Christian writer Hegesippus.[24] After giving a
lengthy description of the ascetic (Essene?) behavior of
James the Just, he tells us that James was accustomed to
discuss the significance of Jesus with representatives of
seven Jewish sects: Essenes, Galileans, Hemerobaptists,
Masbotheans (also baptizers),[25] Samaritans, Sadducees, and
Pharisees. Some converts were made, though in general the
sects did not accept either Jesus' resurrection or his return
as judge. After the death of James, sectarian teaching was
introduced into Jewish Christianity, and thus Gnosticism
arose.

Another early Christian writer, Justin from Samaria, does
not ascribe Gnostic origins to Jewish sects but treats the
two as analogous.[26] His list includes Sadducees, Genistae,
Meristae, Galileans, Hellenians, Pharisees, and Baptists.
Marcel Simon has argued convincingly that Genistae and
Meristae refer to dualistic sects [27] and that the Hellenians are
probably Hellenists.[28]

We must admit that these witnesses are a little late. But
it is difficult to prove that they are necessarily mistaken, or
that Hegesippus' interpretation of Gnosticism as Jewish in
origin is wrong. We should add that the first Gnostic
teacher in whom elements of Hellenistic philosophical
thought are conspicuously present is Basilides, who flourished at Alexandria in the reign of Hadrian (117–138), and

that even in his thought the starting point is not philosophy but revelation, as we shall see (Chapter 5).

If we regard philosophy as providing a vehicle of expression rather than a point of departure (just as in the cases of Philo and Judaism, Plutarch and Egyptian religion, and the apologists and Christianity),[29] we can then inquire whether most of the Iranian elements—specifically, the emphasis on dualism—are not already found in Jewish apocalyptic and especially in the literature produced or preserved at Qumran by the Essenes. Finally, we shall come to the question of Christian influence, and it is at this point that extreme caution will be required, since it would appear that in nearly every case the Gnostic redeemer is the Christian Jesus or is modeled upon him, though the content of his gnosis is not Christian but is somehow related to Judaism.

Before asking any more questions it might be well to turn to some Gnostic systems and try to discover what they have to teach us.

SOME GNOSTIC SYSTEMS

According to Irenaeus the three oldest Gnostic systems are those he ascribes to Simon Magus, Menander, and Saturninus.[30] If we compare the structures of these systems we find remarkable similarities and equally remarkable differences. Both for Simon and for Menander the world was created by angels (archangels, *exousiai*) who had been generated by a first Thought, who in turn had been generated by a first

Power. Saturninus, on the other hand, tells us that the world was created by seven angels (including the God of the Jews) who had been created by the unknown Father. In other words, all three Gnostic teachers retain the Jewish idea of the world as created, not generated, but Simon and Menander speak of generation or emanation in the spiritual world, while Saturninus retains the Jewish doctrine that the heavenly spirits were "made, not begotten."

All three agree that the angelic powers were in rebellion against the supreme power. Simon says that they were eager for authority and that they imprisoned and mistreated the Thought because they were "jealous"—probably a reference to Exodus 20.5. Menander intimates that they brought death into the world, presumably on the ground of Genesis 2–3. And Saturninus says that demons (evil angels) oppressed good men, those who had the spark of life in them, and wanted to destroy the Father; probably he is relying on references to wicked archons in the Psalms. Both Simon and Saturninus state that the Old Testament prophecies were inspired by the angels. Simon specifically says that they gave the Old Testament law, while Saturninus adds that some of the prophecies came from Satan.

All three agree that some savior descended in order to defeat the angels, and that when he descended he did so, though Irenaeus does not tell us how this victory was won. In the Simonian account it was Simon who descended; he appeared to be human, though he was not, and he freed the Thought from her slavery and brought the power of the Jewish law to an end. Menander descended and provided his adherents with a baptism which produced immediate resurrection as well as exemption from old age and death. For Saturninus the Savior was Christ; he merely seemed to be human, and he taught his disciples to avoid marriage and generation, since such customs were instituted by Satan (therefore, at least Genesis 1.28 and 2.18–24 come from Satan). In Saturninus' system the Thought of Simon and Menander has been replaced by the spark of life given to good men. The system has, so to speak, been demythologized; that is to say, one myth has been replaced by another.

If for the moment we disregard the differences among these systems, we find a striking structural similarity. The state of the world as it is is bad, so bad that it can be set right only by divine intervention. Such intervention has now been provided by a savior, whether Simon or Menander or Christ. The bad condition of the world is due to the activity of the evil angels who made it and have since oppressed whatever divine principle remains here below. The wickedness of the angels is to be seen not only in their work of creation but also in their work of inspiring the Old Testament prophets.

Now, if we consider the three cardinal points involved here (angelic creation, angelic inspiration and deception, divine intervention), we find that they represent an extremely heterodox Judaism or even, one might say, Judaism-in-reverse. As far as we can discover, no Jewish teacher ever held that the world was made by angels, though there were those who held that man was made by them.[31] But Jewish teachers did sometimes state that the law was given

through angels,[32] and angels inspire some of the later prophets.[33] Indeed, if we look at the apocalyptic book of Jubilees,
we find that there are mistakes in the Pentateuch which
must be due to some kind of interpolation.

We shall later (in Chapter 2) examine some of the bridges
between apocalyptic Judaism and gnosis, but at this point
we wish only to provide some examples of Jewish Christian
thought which seem to depict stages of development out
of Judaism into Gnosticism. Père Daniélou has recently
shown how much early Christians owed to Jewish speculation and how close many of them came to Gnostic ideas.[34]
Here we give three examples. First we may mention a fragment of an Apocalypse of Zephaniah.[35]

And the Spirit took me up and carried me into the fifth heaven,
and I saw angels, called Lords, and their diadem was lying in
the Holy Spirit, and for each one of them there was a throne
seven times as bright as the light of the rising sun; they dwelt
in temples of salvation and praised the God who is ineffable
and most high.

Here there is nothing which goes beyond apocalyptic;
there are simply the usual ingredients of heavens, angels,
lords, and thrones which Gnostics were ready to mix in
their own way. More significant is the Prayer of Joseph
from which Origen and Eusebius give extracts.[36]

He who speaks to you, I Jacob and Israel, am an angel of God
and a principal (*archikon*) spirit, and Abraham and Isaac were
created before any other work. I Jacob, called Jacob by men,
my name is Israel, I am called by God Israel, the man who sees
God, because I am the first-born (*prōtogonos*) of everything
living which receives its life from God.

When I arrived from Syrian Mesopotamia, the angel of God Uriel came forth and said, "I have descended upon the earth and have tabernacled among men; I was called by the name Jacob." He contended with me and warred with me and struggled against me, saying that his name, which is the Name of him who is before every angel, would raise him over mine. I told him his name and his rank among the sons of God. "Are you not Uriel, the eighth after me, while I am Israel, the archangel of the power of the Lord and the chief tribune among the sons of God? Am I not Israel, the first servant before the face of God?" And I invoked my God by his eternal Name.

Here we find a purely Jewish revelation, but one which is certainly proto-Gnostic because of the rivalry between Jacob-Israel and Uriel. Uriel is both ignorant of and hostile toward the archangel of the power of the Lord. Clearly this fragment represents an attempt to supplant an archangel of the older apocalyptic by a new archangel who makes himself known by a new revelation.

Finally, we may mention a system indubitably Gnostic, that found in the book Baruch composed by a certain Justin.[37] Here the story of creation, sin, and salvation is based on the Old Testament, though foreign elements have been added, notably in the identification of the supreme Good with Priapus, the life-principle, and in the introduction of Heracles as a messenger of Baruch. As an example of a gnosis almost purely Jewish, the system deserves consideration in some detail.

According to Justin, the universe owes its origin to three principles, two male and one female. The first male principle is the cosmic life-giver Priapus; he is the unknown

Father of all. The second, Elohim, is the Father of the universe as it is. He is inferior to the first principle, for he cannot predict the future, and it is only because of him that the universe comes into existence. Elohim sees and desires the third, female, principle, whose name is Eden. Eden returns his love and they produce twenty-four angels, twelve of whom resemble their father, twelve their mother.

How do we know that this story is true? Because in Genesis we read that "Elohim planted a garden in Eden" (2.8), and the garden is obviously the totality of these angels. Individually, they are the trees in the garden. The tree of life is the chief of the angels who resembles Elohim; his name is Baruch, "blessed." The tree of the knowledge of good and evil is the chief maternal angel; his name is Naas, the serpent. And because of their origin all the angels co-operated in making man; Elohim gave him his spirit by breathing into him; Eden gave him his soul. Thus man "became a kind of seal and memorial of their love, and an eternal symbol of the marriage of Eden and Elohim." Afterwards Eve was created too, as a special symbol of Eden herself, and the pair were commanded to "increase and multiply" (Gen. 1.28). Thus, Justin retells the idyllic story of life among the angels, stressing its culmination in marriage. It is "a great mystery" not of Christ and his Church but of creativity and reproduction.

Yet the world is not idyllic. Sin and evil flourish, and the reason for their flourishing lies in the shipwreck of the archetypal marriage. Elohim left Eden to ascend and contemplate the creation, leaving Eden behind since he was spiritual and she was earth. When he had reached what he thought was the top of heaven—we know that he must have ascended in order to see that everything he had made was very good (Gen. 1.31)—he saw a light brighter than the sun. In the words of Psalm 118.19 he said, "Open to me the gates of righteousness, that I may enter and acknowledge the Lord"; and he added a confession of his mistake: "I thought that I was the Lord." The gates were opened, and he entered in; the supreme Good, Priapus, said to him, "Sit at my right hand" (Psalm 110.1).

Now Elohim was so overcome by his new knowledge and exaltation that he asked the Good for permission to destroy the creation he had made and to take back his spirit from men, just as in Genesis Yahweh planned to destroy his creatures (6.7) and said that his spirit would not strive with man forever (6.3). The Good, however, opposed this scheme. He reminded Elohim that nothing which comes ultimately from the Good can be evil. He said, "You and Eden made the world as the result of mutual satisfaction; let Eden have the creation as long as she wants it; you stay with me." So Elohim stayed.

Meanwhile Eden became aware that she had been abandoned by her husband, and therefore made herself more attractive "so that somehow Elohim might come to desire her and return to her." But he did not return. Her love turned to hate and a desire for revenge. She

commanded Babel [Aphrodite] to create adulteries and divorces among men so that, just as she herself was separated from Elohim, the spirit of Elohim in men might be grieved and

tormented and experience the same sufferings as those of the
abandoned Eden. And Eden gave great power to her angel
Naas, so that he could torment the spirit of Elohim in men
with all possible torments, and so that through the spirit Elohim
might be tormented, he who had abandoned his wife in violation of the covenant he had made with her.

Thus both good and evil come from the same action. By departing to the Good, Elohim redeemed himself and showed
the way for those who wish to ascend. But by leaving Eden,
he was the cause of the evils which happen to his spirit in
men. Neither Elohim nor Eden is evil. But both were ignorant; they could not tell what would inevitably happen
as a result of their actions.

The process of redemption for the spirit of Elohim in
man comes about through a series of prophets through
whom Elohim's angel Baruch speaks. These prophets were
Moses and the other Hebrew prophets, Heracles among the
gentiles, and finally Jesus. All but Jesus were unsuccessful
and betrayed their mission; Heracles did so by exchanging
clothing with a snakelike woman who was the servant of
Naas. Jesus, however, was faithful and ascended to the
Good after preaching the gospel of ascent to men.

What kind of system is this? It must be fundamentally
Jewish in origin. Not only the use of Genesis, and of Hebrew names in Genesis, but the whole picture of marriage
and reproduction as the center of human life—these reflect
the Old Testament concentration on marriage and the family. The primary violations of God's plan are seen in adul-

tery and divorce. Yet it is obviously no ordinary Judaism which is reflected here. In the first place, the highest god is above both Elohim, the god of the Old Testament, and Eden, the earth-mother. This is like the mystical Judaism we find in the *Zohar*, where Yahweh is called the Father and Elohim the Mother. But something more has happened when the highest good is called the cosmic Priapus. Foreign mythology has come in, and is reflected again in the choice of Heracles as a prophet of Baruch, as well as in the notion that the twelve angels of Eden correspond to the signs of the zodiac.

What makes the system hold together? It is the Jewish notion that marriage is the foundation of human existence, and that the first of all laws is to increase and multiply. The specific acts of sin which are condemned are adultery and divorce, and pederasty as well. How did they originate? They came out of frustration; and they resulted in more frustration. Human life thus enters a closed circle out of which it can break only by returning to the cosmic good, the life-principle of creativity.

Another idea strikingly Jewish is to be found in the system, for we read in Justin's book that Eden was also Israel.[38] And if we look through the Old Testament for a picture of love somewhat like that in our story, we find it in the Song of Songs, which at least in the first century was being referred to the love of God for Israel.[39] Such an interpretation occurs not only among the rabbis but also among apocalyptic writers: Israel is called "lily," "dove," and "bride" in 2 Esdras (5.24, 26; 7.26). These names are derived from the Song. And a third-century rabbi gives us exegesis which strikingly recalls Justin's system.[40]

"My beloved has gone down into his garden, to the beds of balsam to feed in the gardens to gather lilies" (6.2): "my beloved" is the Holy One, blessed be he; "into his garden," the world; "to the beds of balsam," Israel; "to feed in the gardens," the synagogues and the schools; "to gather lilies," to make ascend the righteous who are in Israel.

This is almost exactly the exegesis we find in Justin, without its Gnostic and syncretistic touches.

And so, when we read that Hosea's marriage signifies "the whole mystery" of the system,[41] we realize that what Justin has done is to work together the rabbinic and apocalyptic—in short, the haggadic—exegesis of Israel as the fallen bride of God, and has created his Gnostic theology largely by changing the names (in rabbinic fashion) and by introducing a little extraneous mythology. In short, as Haenchen suggested, the roots of this system may lie entirely within Judaism, and Heracles may be no more of an addition to it than Jesus is.[42]

Oddly enough, the main outlines of the system recur among anti-Jewish Marcionites in the fifth century, for we find an alternative version of the same myth ascribed to them by the fifth-century Armenian heresiologist Eznik.[43] Here the unknown Father has become "the Stranger"; Elohim is the god of the law; and Eden is Hylé (matter). The god of the law descended after creation, and he and

Hylé made man together. Hylé provided clay and the god of the law gave spirit; they placed Adam and his wife in the garden described in the law. So far the story is the same as that in Baruch. But then the Marcionites went on to describe a conflict between the god of the law and Hylé, from whom he stole Adam. Thereafter Hylé made many gods (the angels of Baruch), who led Adam's offspring astray, while the god of the law cast into Gehenna those who were leaving their bodies, as well as Adam, after he ate from the tree of knowledge. This criticism of the creator is of course Marcionite. Finally, the Good Stranger sent his Son, who, after being crucified, emptied hell, thus causing the god of the law to tear his mantle and the veil of his temple and to darken the sun. Once more, Jesus descended, this time in the form of his deity, to contend with the god of the law; this time he won. He took Paul and revealed to him the purchase price, and Paul preached that everyone who believes in Jesus has been sold by the just (god of the law) to the Good.

In this story the Jewish elements found in Justin have been excised. The angels play no part; after creation they ascend with the god of the law to heaven but never return. The picture of matter as Eden and Israel is gone. The prophets and their missions are absent. Jesus is the Son of the Good Stranger, not a prophet sent by Baruch. And Paul, not mentioned by Justin, is the true apostle of the Good.

This interpretation of the story shows how myths Jewish-

Christian in origin could be externally Hellenized (Hylé) and heretically Christianized. Both forms are Gnostic, but the earlier is the more Jewish.

We have seen that some, at least, of the most significant early Gnostic systems have Jewish roots. This is not to say that Gnosticism should be regarded as Jewish. None of the Gnostic leaders we know has a Jewish name, and rabbinic teachers, in their struggle against the Minim in the second and third centuries, make clear how abhorrent dualistic doctrines are. At the same time it must be admitted that rabbinic teachers do not fully reflect the varieties of religious experience to be found within Judaism before the fall or falls of Jerusalem; there is a great deal of dualism in apocalyptic literature, even though the supremacy of God is maintained. But Gnostics go beyond apocalyptic thought. The Gnostic teachers may have regarded themselves as the only true Jews, but certainly authoritative rabbinic teachers did not regard them so.[44] For all practical purposes the Gnostics must have been ex-Jews, renegades from their religion, for they had abandoned the deity of the Creator, the binding character of the law of Moses, and the doctrine of resurrection.

Our problem now is to try to determine the circumstances under which such an abandonment of basic Jewish principles could arise. This means that we must say something about the development of the apocalyptic-eschatological hope.

THE APOCALYPTIC-ESCHATOLOGICAL HOPE

For our purposes we must simplify the story. We shall venture upon a kind of "reductionism," treating the history as an expression of basic attitudes toward historical experience. This may have the merit of making the story comprehensible to modern students. At any rate, it will perhaps make it more comprehensible to ourselves.

It would appear that we should first differentiate apocalyptic from prophetic thought. The Old Testament prophets, generally speaking, are convinced of two things. In the first place, their nation is in a bad condition. In the second place, God is going to act in order to correct this situation. The prophets do not know just when God is going to do so; they know only that he is going to act. Apocalyptic writers are more pessimistic about the world and more confident, at least on the surface, about the imminence of God's action. Many of them expect that God will destroy the world and substitute a new one for the old. Many of them believe that they can predict not only God's action but the approximate time in which he will act.

In the apocalyptic book of Daniel, the struggle of the Jewish people against Antiochus Epiphanes is given divine sanction. The book sets forth a schedule of future events and explains exactly when God is going to produce the victory of "the people of the saints of the Most High." Apocalyptic writing was given confirmation, seemingly miraculous, when the schedule turned out to be nearly cor-

rect. Not all Jews, however, regarded the success of the
Maccabean family as approved by God. There were those
who withdrew their support from the hereditary royal
priesthood and removed themselves to the seclusion of Qumran by the Dead Sea. There they produced their own apocalypses, which predicted the intervention of God on behalf
of their sect, not on behalf of the Jewish people as a whole.
Gradually their attitude was transformed from simple
apocalyptic prediction, as in Enoch, Jubilees, and the Testament of Levi, to advocacy of a holy war, to be waged by
themselves, the "sons of light," against all others, the
"sons of darkness." In other words, among this kind of
apocalyptic thinkers there arose something like the attitude
of the later Zealots. "Hope long deferred maketh the heart
sick."

In the first century of our era apocalyptic expectation
and efforts to realize the expectation were often combined.
In A.D. 6, after the ethnarch of Judaea had been deposed
by the Romans, a certain Judas arose in Galilee to oppose
the payment of taxes to Rome and to establish a the-
ocracy—in other words, rule by himself and his allies.[45] He
may have regarded the Roman effort to take a census as
the work of Satan, for in 1 Chronicles 21.1 it is stated that
Satan was behind David's attempts along the same lines. In
the time of Jesus there were similar expectations. Many of
his disciples, as Luke points out, supposed that the reign of
God was going to appear immediately (19.11), or "hoped
that it was he who would redeem Israel" (24.21), or expected him to "restore the kingdom to Israel" (Acts 1.6).

Under Caligula, a few years later, there were fears that the "abomination of desolation" (Mark 13.14; Daniel 9.27)—a colossal statue of the emperor as Zeus [46]—would be placed in the temple, but the Roman governor of Syria was able to temporize until the emperor's death; thus the crisis was averted. Under Claudius, at the time of a famine in Judaea, an enthusiast named Theudas gathered his followers by the Jordan river and told them that he could make the waters part so they could march across. The Romans beheaded him before the miracle could be worked.[47] Under Nero, the Jewish high priest was murdered, and "prophets" arose who persuaded many to go out into the desert to view God's "signs of freedom." Again, Roman troops killed most of them. A prophet came from Egypt to lead four thousand Jews from the wilderness to the Mount of Olives. He told them that at his command the walls of Jerusalem would fall and they could take the city. Once more, Roman troops anticipated the apocalyptic event.[48]

About the year 62 the long-awaited signs began to be given in Jerusalem itself. Before the feast of Passover a miraculous light illuminated the altar in the temple. Several weeks later, chariots and armed soldiers were seen in the clouds. At Pentecost the priests heard the sound of many voices saying, "We are departing hence." And at Tabernacles a rustic named Joshua pronounced apocalyptic woes against Jerusalem and the temple.[49] Four years later the revolt against Rome finally began in earnest, in spite of the efforts of the aristocracy to prevent it. In the course of the war religious motives were prominent. Zealots

murdered the high priest and proceeded to appoint high
priests of their own, choosing them by lot according to ancient custom.[50] Like the Essenes, the Zealots detested the
hereditary high priesthood of the Hasmoneans. Essenes
were active in the war—one of the Jewish generals was
John the Essene [51]—and Josephus tells us how the Essenes
died when they had been made prisoners by the Romans.[52]
Signs from heaven were given during the war. A swordlike
star stood over the city, and a comet appeared throughout
a year's time.[53] Perhaps the star was the one "out of Jacob,"
foretold in Numbers (24.17) and looked for by the Dead
Sea group.[54] At the very end of the war there were prophets
in Jerusalem who urged to the people to climb to the roof
of the temple, where God would give them miraculous
signs of deliverance.[55]

In spite of all this religious enthusiasm, Vespasian burned
Qumran, probably in the summer of 68, and in 70 Jerusalem itself fell and the temple was destroyed by fire. Apocalyptic faith survived the catastrophe for a while. At Alexandria revolutionary leaders still urged Jews to assert their
liberty, to view the Romans as no better than themselves,
and to look upon God as their only master. The revolt was
suppressed by the Romans.[56] In Cyrene a weaver led one
more group of visionaries into the desert to see "signs and
portents"; they were dispersed by the Romans.[57]

In this long and tragic chain of events, apocalyptic hopes
were extremely important. When they continued to be
shattered, not only at the fall of Jerusalem but also earlier,

severe religious readjustments must have been necessary. Such revisions must have been made by other groups as well. Three examples can be provided. (1) When Tiridates, king of Armenia, received his diadem from Nero in the year 66, he brought Magi with him to Rome and hailed Nero with a formula of "eschatological recognition": "I have come to thee my god, worshiping thee as I do Mithra; thou art my Fate and my Fortune." [58] Two years later, when Nero committed suicide, some explanation must have been needed. (2) In the Orient there were other enthusiasts, perhaps relying on an apocalypse ascribed to the ancient Persian king Hystaspes, who believed that a world-ruler was about to arise from their midst.[59] For a moment it looked as if their hopes would be fulfilled; but then Vespasian and Titus consolidated Roman power once more. Some orientals then claimed that Nero had not really died and that he would return to lead the East against the West.[60] The more realistic Josephus argued that Jewish prophecy, at least, had been fulfilled by Vespasian,[61] but it is most unlikely that all Jews shared his confidence. (3) When the Capitol at Rome was burned in 69, Druid prophets in Gaul regarded the fire as a sign from heaven, indicating that Gaul, not Rome, was about to become the ruler of the world.[62] Their expectations, like those of others, were not fulfilled.

Not all Jews gave up their hope of divine intervention. We meet it again in the fourth book of the Sibylline Oracles, in 2 Esdras, and in the Jewish Christian Apocalypse

of John. In Syria there arose the prophet Elchasai, given a
revelation by colossal angels and predicting a great eschatological struggle on the Syrian-Parthian border.[63]

Elchasai's prediction, proclaimed toward the end of the
first century, was fulfilled in 115, when the emperor Trajan
was busy with a war in Mesopotamia. A Jewish revolt
broke out in Cyrene and soon spread to Egypt and Cyprus,
then to Palestine and Mesopotamia itself. This extremely
violent and bloody revolt was put down only in 117.
Around this time Roman soldiers erected a votive altar for
Serapis in Jerusalem.[64] Once more, apocalyptic expectations had to be revised. The author of 2 Baruch rewrote 2
Esdras in order to bring it up to date. While 2 Esdras had
held that universal sin brought about the fall of Jerusalem,
2 Baruch apparently held that the most recent revolt failed
because its leaders were sinners.

Did apocalyptic enthusiasm come to an end? Certainly
not. Only fifteen years later, the emperor Hadrian an-
nounced his intention of building a new Greek city on the
site of Jerusalem, and of erecting a temple of Jupiter Capi-
tolinus there. A certain Simon bar Koseba raised the standard of revolt,[65] and the famous Jewish rabbi Akiba was
willing to regard him as the star arising out of Jacob. He
called him Bar Kochba ("son of the star"). The hopeless
revolt lasted three and a half years, apparently because Bar
Kochba, or his theological adviser, believed that victory in
that time was foretold in the book of Daniel. According to
Dio Cassius, more than half a million Jews lost their lives.[66]

This event marks the effective end of ancient Jewish apocalypticism.[67]

We have already seen that in all these revolts against Rome both religious and political motives were interwoven. The interweaving is expressed on the coins struck by the Jewish rebels. From the first revolt we possess coins inscribed "Jerusalem the Holy" and "deliverance of Zion"; from the second, we may mention those which bear a star, the name Simon, and the words "for the freedom of Jerusalem." [68] In both revolts the coins were dated from the beginning of the wars; the establishment of an independent state presumably implied the arrival of the reign of God.

But to the Jewish revolutionary coins there correspond the Roman issues with the legend "Judaea Capta." [69] In the first war the temple was burned and rendered unusable; in the second it was practically demolished. God had given no sign that he would deliver his people, and he had not acted in support of the sectarians of Qumran. Marmorstein has cited rabbinical texts which strongly suggest that many Jews came to doubt the cardinal attributes of God: his omnipotence, his omniscience, and his providential care.[70]

And it was under these circumstances that the later apocalyptic writers, as Buber has observed, lost their faith in a genuine historical future. "Everything here is predetermined; all human decisions are only sham struggles." He explains this development in general terms. "Wherever man shudders before the menace of his own work and wishes to flee from the radically demanding historical hour, there he finds himself near [to] the apocalyptic vision of a process that cannot be arrested." [71]

Not only apocalyptic enthusiasts, but Jews in general, must have had their faith shaken. The temple services had come to an end; what were priests and levites to do? With the temple destroyed, how could pious Pharisees continue to obey the law of Moses? With the failure of the apocalyptic vision, how could it be maintained by either Essenes or Zealots? The law and the prophets remained; but how were they to be interpreted? It was under these circumstances that the author of 2 Baruch could write, "I see many of thy people who have left thy covenant and have put aside the yoke of thy law" (41.3). Even earlier, in a speech ascribed to a Zealot leader, Josephus refers to the temple as once "believed to have God as its inhabitant." [72] Faith was shaken in God, his covenant, his law, and his promises.

Out of such shaking, we should claim, came the impetus toward Gnostic ways of thinking, doubtless not for the first time with the fall of Jerusalem but reinforced by this catastrophe. Two modern parallels may perhaps serve as illustrations of the process. (1) Like the Jews in the Roman empire, the Plains Indians were a "subordinate ethnic group" in nineteenth-century America. When their warfare failed, their traditional culture "became inadequate and disorganized." Under these circumstances, "the usual symptoms of social maladjustment appeared: preoccupation with the problem situation, questioning of custom, social unrest, increased nonconformity, breakdown of social con-

trols, social disorganization, and personality maladjustment." [73] The same difficulties are to be found among most
Gnostics. (2) Very recently in Utah studies were made of
a small group which anticipated a cosmic catastrophe and
the arrival of space ships to rescue believers; after nothing
happened the reaction of some of them, at least, was fairly
Gnostic in expression.[74]

When his predictions were not realized, the apocalypti-
cist of the first century had several options. (1) He could
postpone the time of fulfillment and rewrite his apocalypse;
such revisions were actually made. (2) He could abandon
his religion entirely. (3) He could look for escape rather
than victory, and could then reinterpret his sacred writings
in order to show that the revelation had been misunderstood. It would appear that most Gnostic teachers did reinterpret not only the Old Testament but also some of
the apocalyptic writings or their ingredients, as we shall
see in Chapter 2. The essence of their religion had come
to be knowledge of the nature of the self and of the way in
which the self could escape from this world to another.
The nature of the other world could be understood in the
light of the apocalypses.

There is one more ingredient in Gnosticism, however,
which is indispensable or nearly indispensable. It is symbolically expressed in the words of Simon Peter (John
6.68): "Lord, to whom shall we go? You have words of
eternal life." A would-be Gnostic, searching for security in
a troubled and evil world, could hardly ignore the claims
being made for Jesus by Christians, though the emphasis

laid on apocalyptic eschatology by many of them would hardly appeal to him. In view of the diversity of views about Jesus, the Gnostic might well claim that just as he knew the true meaning of the Old Testament so he, and he alone, knew the true meaning of Jesus. As we shall see when we consider various Gnostic systems, it is highly probable that in all of them it is Jesus who is either the Savior or the model for the gnostic savior. Exceptions to this rule may be provided in early oriental Simonianism, if it can be reconstructed (see Chapter 3)—but it was not really Gnostic—and in such philosophical Gnosticizing movements as those represented in the *Hermetica* and the *Chaldaean Oracles*—but these writings are less Gnostic than philosophical (see Chapter 5).

It seems to me that earlier stages of a similar process can be detected in the thought of the apostle Paul. His message to the Greco-Roman world was originally apocalyptic; in his Thessalonian letters we see him trying to correct the exaggerated idea that the day of the Lord has already come (2 Thess. 2.2). Later he modifies his views and the emphasis on apocalyptic diminishes while proto-Gnostic ideas are expressed. Similarly the Fourth Evangelist reinterprets the Gospel, translating it into terms close to what Gnostic thought became. For this reason the apocalyptic-eschatological expression "the kingdom of God" is infrequent in both Paul and John. Later Gnostics had high regard for both writers.

I should not claim that everything in gnosis can be explained as due to the failure of Jewish apocalyptic hopes.

All I should claim is that the failure of apocalyptic led to the rise of new forms of religious expression in which the old, while still present, was transposed and transformed. When Jonas defines gnosis as "anti-cosmic and eschatological dualism," it seems to me that the eschatological dualism is Jewish (and ultimately Iranian) in origin, while the anti-cosmic aspect arises out of a belief that the God of this cosmos has failed to act on behalf of his people. Apocalyptic writers had already laid tremendous emphasis on the badness of the world, but they expected God's intervention. They had speculated about the heavens above and the angelic and demonic powers which dwelt in them. When their hope of immediate victory was denied, they recognized themselves as strangers and afraid in a world their God had never made. Two kinds of Jews were affected with this despair. Palestinian enthusiasts for apocalyptic were more directly affected, but Hellenized Jews in the Diaspora cannot have remained untouched. Some doubtless became Christians; the use of Philo by Clement of Alexandria may suggest that he had prospective converts at least partly in view. Others used the allegorical method to find gnosis in the Old Testament, and in the Christian writings as well. Both Palestinian and Hellenistic Jews espoused the doctrine of "two powers" condemned by rabbinic teachers.

We cannot insist that everything in Gnosticism can be explained in relation to Jewish apocalyptic hopes. Certainly, by the second generation of Gnostic believers we find a great deal of concern with revelations mediated through ancient oriental teachers, through early Greeks, in short, through ancient theology of every sort.[75] The Simonians and the Naassenes, for example, devote a good deal of time to giving exegesis of Homer.[76] And the Christian element in Gnosticism must not be neglected. At the same time, as we examine various early systems we shall find reinforcement for the hypothesis that Gnosticism originates out of the failure of the apocalyptic hope. Père Daniélou and others have claimed that "ontological dualism" is what differentiates Gnosticism from Judaism or from Jewish Christianity.[77] I should agree in maintaining this distinction, but while others have claimed that Gnosticism is "Greek" in origin, I should be inclined, in view of (1) the nonphilosophical nature of Gnosticism and (2) the relative rarity of this kind of dualism among Hellenistic philosophers, to claim that it originates from historical experience. To be sure, the expression of the meaning found in the historical experience may owe something to reflections of philosophy, if not to philosophical reflection; but to ascribe any large measure of philosophical thought to the Gnostics seems an unnecessary hypothesis.

In the period when Gnosticism arose, apocalyptic-minded Jews might have sought signs of the Creator's power and his intervention on their behalf; philosophically minded Greeks might have looked for speculative wisdom, more or less rational in nature; but the Gnostic preached himself and his true spiritual origin, both of which he had come to know by revelation.

2

THE HEAVENLY WORLD

SINCE we are now committed to the thesis that Gnosticism originated out of apocalyptic Judaism, it is time to provide some evidence which may prove to support this view. There is no need to go into the origins or the historical setting of the apocalyptic movement, or even into the history of the Dead Sea community at Qumran. All we need say is that according to our theory nearly all the ingredients later found in Gnosticism were already present in the life and the literature of these Essenes or near-Essenes. What happened when the apocalyptic movement came to be transmuted into gnosis was that the hope of justification, of sanctification, of redemption, of vindication by God in this world and in this period of time was lost. What had formerly been meaningful in relation to a calendar to be observed was transferred to the starry heavens. The dualistic elements already present in apocalyptic thought were magnified, and the element of free choice, already on the wane, came to be almost completely lost. The world, formerly the battleground of good and evil men and angels, came to be viewed as the product of evil angels from whose power only escape could be provided—escape through the planetary spheres they governed to the supreme but alien God above.

THE CALENDAR

We know that among the Dead Sea sectarians great emphasis was laid upon the importance of observing the correct calendar, known to the sectarians by divine revelation and maintained in opposition to the calendar in use at Jerusalem. Their *Manual of Discipline* insists upon the observance of such a time scheme. God is to be blessed only in accordance with it.[1]

Upon examining these calendars we find in both of them that "the prevalent system of fixing the festivals by the first appearance of the new moon, and trying to adjust the lunar cycle of months to the solar cycle of seasons," has been abandoned.[2] Instead, the basic division is one into four seasons, each of which has three months of thirty days each, and one extra day. Each season thus lasts 91 days, and the year consists of 12 months and 4 seasonal days, a total of 52 weeks of 7 days each, or 364 days. This total has been given the apocalyptic writers by divine inspiration. Today we are aware that this is not the length of the solar year, and in antiquity, especially in the Hellenistic age, calendars were often created containing 365 or even 365¼ days. But it should be observed that the calendar of Enoch and Jubilees would go wrong only gradually; it would take about 24½ years for it to be a month off; and when it got to be two months off one might have thought a year of Jubilee had arrived.

These books also pay considerable attention to the week, since for a long time the Jews had been observing the Sabbath. This seven-day period seems to be Jewish in origin (perhaps related to Babylonian models), but in the late Hellenistic age it came to be known throughout the Greek and Roman world, and there was correlated with the seven planets, each of which had its special day.[3]

One may wonder what all this has to do with Gnosticism. In the previous chapter we suggested that Gnosticism, or rather the impetus for Gnostic thinking, came from the debris of shattered eschatological hopes. Now we shall try to show that in the debris were calendrical notions which were transformed into Gnostic theologoumena.

Before doing so we should say something about the use of apocalyptic literature among the Gnostics. This is not always easy to demonstrate. Origen suggests that a Gnostic doctrine known to Celsus came from the book of Enoch;[4] in *Pistis Sophia* we read that the *Books of Ieû* were written by Enoch in paradise;[5] and the later Manichees and Bogomils used both 1 Enoch and 2 Enoch.[6] The Ascension of Isaiah, part of which may have originated at Qumran,[7] was used by the Archontics.[8] More significant is the way in which the apocalypse form flourished in various Gnostic sects. Many of the books found at Nag-Hammadi are apocalypses—one of Adam to Seth, one of Dositheus, one of Sêém or the Great Seth. The Gnostic Justin wrote a

book called Baruch, presumably because he knew something of the tradition in which revelations were ascribed to
the Old Testament personage (though for Justin Baruch
has become an angel). [9]

With or without written sources, however, it appears
that when the Gnostics were concerned with what separated them from the supreme deity they made use of
materials calendrical in origin in order to find out what it
was. For this reason they were concerned with groups of
four (the seasons), of seven (the planetary week), and of
thirty (the lunar month). We shall examine these groups in
this order and then go on to see how the Father or the chief
of the seven came to be regarded as the enemy of mankind.

THE FOUR LIGHTS

In post-exilic Judaism we first encounter the archangels of
God. Their number varies: sometimes there are seven,
sometimes there are six, sometimes there are four. Similarly,
in Iranian thought there were variations, and the minister-
ing spirits of Ahura Mazda, like those of Ahriman, were
sometimes seven and sometimes six. The notion that four
among the seven or six were predominant seems to arise out
of speculation related to the four sides of the throne of
God, with which the archangels were related, as well as
from consideration of the four corners of the earth and
perhaps the four seasons of the year.

We know the names of three of the archangels from the
larger canon of the Old Testament: they are Michael,

Gabriel, and Raphael. But it was obviously necessary to identify the fourth, and in 1 Enoch he is sometimes called Uriel, sometimes Phanuel. Michael and Gabriel recur in the New Testament. In the Dead Sea War Scroll three names are preserved out of four; they are Michael, Sariel, and Raphael. In all this Jewish and Jewish Christian literature the archangels are servants of God. Similarly, in an Ophite list copied by Celsus the first four angels who serve the Creator are Michael, Suriel, Raphael, and Gabriel.

When we turn to other Gnostic literature, we find in the Apocryphon of John that in consequence of a union between the aeons Christ and Imperishability four luminaries were emitted. They now stand about an aeon named Autogenes and illuminate the spiritual world. Only one of them, however, can be identified with any of the four archangels we know; this is Oroiael, presumably identical with Uriel. His name is given by Irenaeus as Raguel—and Raguel is one of the seven archangels named in the book of Enoch. The other three are Harmozel (Armogen), Daveithe (David), and Eleleth.[10]

The names of the four, then, do not exactly coincide with those of the archangels. But in Enoch there are not only archangels but also great lights which represent seasonal aspects of the sun. These are Meleial, "fulness of God" (autumn); Narel or Oriares, "lamp of God" or "light of the sun" (winter); Milkiel, "my God is king" (spring); and Elimelech, "my king is God" (summer).[11] The correspondence between Oriares and Oroiael or Uriel is obvious. But if we consider the kingship mentioned in Enoch's list we may suggest that the Old Testament king most emphasized by apocalyptic writers is David, and that a transportation has taken place here as apocalyptic was transmuted into gnosis.

Further correspondences can be discovered when we consider that in Enoch the seasonal names are accompanied by angelic names related to the months. Thus with Milkiel are associated Barkiel, "blessed of God," and Zabesael, "this is God's heart," and with Elimelech, Keel, perhaps "unto God," and Heel, "God lives." The same situation obtains in gnosis. David, for example, has satellites, and among them are "understanding" and "love." It seems significant that in Hebrew "understanding" is דעת, while "love," at least in the Song of Songs, is related to the root דוד. The correlations suggest that the starting point of the speculations lies in apocalyptic concern for the calendar, while it has then passed into Gnostic emanationism.

We have still not left the archangels entirely behind, for an old rabbinic allegorization tells us that "the throne of God has four standards: righteousness, justice, grace, and truth" [12]—and both grace and truth are found in various lists of the satellites of the four great lights.

A similar combination of motifs occurs in a full list now available in The Sacred Book of the Great Invisible Spirit found at Nag-Hammadi.[13] The lights are those we have found in the Apocryphon of John: Harmozel, Oroiael, Daveithe, and (H)Eleleth. With them are associated "grace," "sense-perception," "understanding," and "foresight." But this is not all. We find two more lists, which include, first, Gamaliel, Gabriel, Samlo, and Abrasax and, second, "memory," "love," "peace," and "eternal life." What a conglomeration! Can we make any sense out of these combinations?

Harmozel—grace—Gamaliel—memory
Oroiael—sense-perception—Gabriel—love
Daveithe—understanding—Samlo—peace
Eleleth—foresight—Abrasax—eternal life

The trouble with trying to do so is that all the sense we can make is partial. For instance, grace goes well with Gamaliel, since Gamaliel means "benefit of God." But what do they have to do with memory? Gabriel means "man of God" and as an archangel is often associated with Uriel; but there seems to be no relation with, or between, sense-perception and love. Samlo, as Campbell Bonner pointed out,[14] contains the consonants of the Hebrew word for "peace," but other correlations are hard to find. And in the case of Abrasax and eternal life we may perhaps suspect that intentional mystification is going on.

Therefore, we may proceed to a further conclusion. What made sense in its original calendrical-apocalyptic setting no longer makes much sense transferred to the realm of gnosis. The process is like that which transformed "Hoc est corpus meum" into "hocus-pocus." Not everything in gnosis is deeply meaningful.

We should not suggest, of course, that such ideas are to be found only in apocalyptic or Gnostic thought. Thirty years ago Erik Peterson wrote of "der viereinige Gott in der iranisch-chaldäischen Theologie," and showed how

Greco-Roman theologians, relying on Oriental sources, identified various gods with the four seasons and then spoke of the unity of the four.[15] Thus the formula, "One is Zeus Hades Helios Dionysos (Sarapis, Iao)," refers to the perennial unity of spring, summer, autumn, and winter; so does the formula, "Abraxas Soter Bel Iao." Here the presence of Abraxas and Iao is especially significant in relation to our Gnostic formulas (if the text of Hyginus has been correctly restored),[16] but Soter is important too, since Irenaeus tells us that the great light Armogen (Harmozel) is also called Soter.

The Gnostic analysis of the four lights, then, probably goes back to some form of "Iranian-Chaldaean theology," and it was mediated to Gnostics through apocalyptic Judaism, even though it is possible, and indeed probable, that in the course of Gnostic development Iranian and Chaldaean thought exercised further direct influence. At the beginning, however, we should claim that apocalyptic Judaism provided the sources of this idea.

THE SEVEN SPIRITS

In gnosis we find not only the four lights but also a group of seven spirits, either including the creator-god or subordinate to him. Such spirits obviously resemble the seven archangels of the Jewish apocrypha and pseudepigrapha. We encounter them in Tobit, in the Testament of Levi, in the literature related to Enoch, and in the Apocalypse of John. In this Jewish or Jewish Christian literature the seven are subordinate to the good Creator; they are not hostile either to him or to mankind. This is the crucial difference between apocalyptic and Gnostic thought: for Gnostics the angelic powers are hostile both to the supreme god and to men. But in the book of Enoch we read that the planets are to be punished for transgressing the commandment of the Lord (18.12–16; 21.1–6), and in the Jewish Christian Testament of Reuben (2.2; 3.2–6) we find seven spirits of deceit which oppress mankind. The way was thus prepared for the notion of a group of seven spirits hostile to mankind and planetary in nature.

We seem to be able to trace a development from apocalyptic to Gnostic thought even within two lists of the seven which Origen supplies from Ophite sources. In the first, their names are Michael, Suriel, Raphael, Gabriel, Thauthabaoth, Erathaoth, and Onoel or Thartharaoth.[17] This list is obviously Jewish in origin; the first four names belong to the four great archangels about the throne of God. But it has been expanded in what we may call a pseudo-Hebrew manner. Almost certainly the last name T(h)art(h)araoth, is a Hebraized form of Tartarus,[18] and we may conjecture that Thauthabaoth is a variant form of the Tohu and Bohu which we meet in the Old Testament.[19] In the second list we find a thoroughly Gnosticized picture, for here the names are Ialdabaoth, Iao, Sabaoth, Adonai, Astaphaeus, Ailoaeus, and Horaeus.[20] Here names or attributes of God in the Old Testament are assigned to various planetary angels; Astaphaeus is perhaps a variant form of the name Satan. Once again, however, the way has been prepared in apocalyptic literature, where we first encounter Sabaoth as a name of God.[21]

But we learn more from Origen than the names of the spirits. We learn formulas by which they could be addressed as the divine element within man ascended through them to the supreme deity above them. And we learn that they were related to the various planets, and that each one of them bore the head or mask of an animal. This information is roughly confirmed by the Apocryphon of John.

	Celsus	Origen I	Origen II	Apocryphon (pp. 41–42)
1	lion	Michael—lion	Ialdabaoth	Ialdabaoth—lion—
2	bull	Suriel—bull	Iao	snake (37, 21)
3	"hissing"	Raphael—snake	Sabaoth	Iaoth—lion
4	eagle	Gabriel—eagle	(Adonai)	Eloaios—ass
5	bear	Thauthabaoth—bear	Astaphaeus	Astaphaios—hyena
6	dog	Erathaoth—dog	Ailoaeus	Iao—snake (7 heads)
7	ass	Thartharaoth—ass	Horaeus	Adoni—ape
				Sabbataios—fire

Professor G. Scholem has drawn my attention to an Ophite amulet on which both Jewish and Gnostic appellations are present. On it there is a lion-headed god, with the name IALDABAOTH on one side of him and the name AARIEL (Hebrew, "lion of God") on the other.[22] Once more we are on the borderline between Judaism and Gnosticism.

But we cannot be content to say that the end product is Gnostic without inquiring what kind of theological influence made this kind of gnosis what it was. And at this point it seems undeniable that somehow or other Gnostic thought owes a great deal to Iranian teaching about Ahriman, the opponent of Ahura Mazda. From exactly this

period we possess the testimony of Plutarch, who tells us
that Areimanios created six gods hostile to Ahura Mazda
and his allies.[23] The number varies; in other texts we read
that "the seven planets are said to be the seven commanders
on the side of Ahriman."[24] The same inconsistency is
found both in apocalyptic and in Gnostic thought. Sometimes Ialdabaoth creates six archons of which he is the chief,
and then he is identified with the planetary deity Saturn;
sometimes he creates seven and rules over them all.[25] It
would appear that Ahriman as Satan is the prototype of
Ialdabaoth. Another striking resemblance can be found in
what Plutarch tells us of Ahriman. He "resembles darkness and ignorance"; indeed, he can be called "darkness."[26]
And in the Apocryphon of John, Ialdabaoth is an ignorant
god, who is called "the first archon of darkness."[27]

But what of the fact that in the Apocryphon he has the
form of a lion and a snake (p. 37.21)? Such a description
immediately calls to mind the innumerable statues found
outside Mithraic shrines, lion-headed human figures within
the coils of a snake. Franz Cumont identified this personage
with Endless Time (αἰών) and claimed that he stood for
the Iranian Zurvan.[28] And Bousset drew attention to his resemblance to Ialdabaoth.[29] But not everyone has agreed that
he was either Aion or Zurvan. I have neither competence
nor inclination to enter into the history of Zurvanism, but
several points seem clear at this stage of the debate. No
matter what the monster may have meant to Iranians—and
in any event his creation may be due to Egyptians [30]—by
the time Gnostics took interest in him he was identified as

Ahriman. As Duchesne-Guillemin points out, Ahriman "is the only Iranian god, except for Mithra, whose name was transmitted to the Occident." [31]

Admittedly the identification of the monster with Ahriman by Legge,[32] Duchesne-Guillemin,[33] and Zaehner [34] has encountered a good deal of criticism, notably by Pettazoni and Mary Boyce.[35] But at least it seems clear that gnostics *could* have made a similar identification. And Celsus, who investigated Ophite affairs in the second century, was probably right when he compared their diagrams and passwords with a Mithraic planetary ladder.[36]

How far toward Mithraism should one go in analyzing the planetary angels? Perhaps we shall do better remaining as far as possible within the orbit of Jewish influence, even with regard to the Apocryphon of John. We might suppose that the hyena is related to Astaphaios because it was highly regarded by the Magi,[37] but it is more likely that the names and the animals are to be correlated on the basis of Aramaic words. Iaoth does not mean "lion," but he is replacing the Michael of earlier Jewish lists. Eloi is presumably related to the word עיל, "ass." Astaphaios-hyena and Sabbataios-fire have been mixed up, for אשתא means "fire" and צבוע means "hyena." Adoni-ape goes well with אדני השדה, which Dalman translates as "Name eines wunderbaren Geschöpfes, vielleicht Orang Utang." [38] We are then left with only Iao-snake and Adonaios-snake, both presumably derived from Ophite doctrine.

We have now said enough about the animals, so we therefore turn to the relation of the seven to the planets.

The Apocryphon tells us explicitly that Ialdabaoth set them to rule over the heaven, and that they constitute the hebdomad of the week.[39] This means that in the Apocryphon, at any rate, we can identify them with the various planets which rule over the various days; the seventh, Sabbataios, must correspond with Saturday. If we try to arrange them in another order, that of their presumed distances from the earth, we find that the lists of the seven given in other documents work out fairly well. They do not work out exactly. Presumably copyists, both Gnostic and Christian, tended to get a bit weary as they went through the lists.

What we have now seen in dealing with the seven is that while their names are Jewish, their functions are much more closely associated with Iranian thought, and both Egyptian and Iranian influence is further suggested by their possession of the heads of animals. As we go farther into the heavenly world we shall encounter further examples of such syntheses. One would suppose that in the period before the creation of the gnostic systems we know, Iranian thought had so strongly influenced Judaism as to transform it. More precisely, those whose faith in Judaism had been shaken welcomed revision from the East.

THE THIRTY AEONS

The four great lights correspond to the four seasons; the seven planetary powers correspond to the days of the week. Now we must consider the thirty heavenly aeons in the

Valentinian Pleroma. They came into existence in this way: First two aeons produced two more; then the second pair produced another pair, and so on until there were eight. The fifth and sixth then produced ten aeons, and the seventh and eighth produced twelve. Now the sum of 8, 10, and 12 is 30. But why were ten produced after the first four? The Valentinian answer to this question is that the sum of 1, 2, 3, and 4 is 10. Then why were twelve produced? This is the sum of 2, 4, and 6. And why thirty in all? It is the sum of 2, 4, 6, 8, and 10.[40]

These answers are not especially satisfactory. They look as if they were concocted to explain a figure already reached on other grounds, and we shall probably not be wrong if we assume that the total of thirty is related to the number of days in the ideal lunar month. Bousset pointed to a late Zoroastrian statement that in addition to Ahura Mazda and Ahriman, and four gods below them, there are "twenty-four other gods, making a total of thirty, in accordance with the days of the month." [41] But we do not need to look quite so far afield. The Valentinians themselves state that the thirty correspond to the days of the lunar month,[42] and such a month is found among the Essenes, in the books of Enoch and Jubilees.[43]

Another significant detail shows the relation of Valentinian thought to Judaism. According to the Valentinians, the first eight aeons, the Ogdoad, can be found in the book of Genesis, where Beginning, God, Heaven, and Earth are mentioned first, then Abyss, Darkness, Water, and Spirit. Then Genesis goes on to mention twenty-two works of creation, making a total of thirty.[44] Now the striking thing is that the book of Jubilees also carefully points out that the works created by God on the six days of creation are twenty-two in number.[45] The Valentinians have translated creation by emanation, and have transferred the scene from this universe to the one above.

Unfriendly critics have noticed that there is a considerable gap between the account of the thirty aeons above and that of the origin of the phenomenal world. Valentinians explained the latter as due to the fall of the thirtieth aeon, Sophia, but her motive in falling is never made quite clear. If the world of aeons above is perfect, it is hard to see why the world below is so bad. Perhaps we can explain the badness of the world below by considering the calendar once more. When Sophia fell from the perfect world, she left only twenty-nine aeons in it, and it is no longer perfect. Her fall may therefore explain why nowadays there are often twenty-nine days in a lunar month rather than thirty. In the book of Enoch only half of the months have thirty days; the rest have twenty-nine.[46] When we press the question further and ask why the phenomenal world should be regarded as bad, we may recall what Enoch says about his divinely inspired calendar. If it does not work properly —and it does not—the maladjustment is due solely to human sin.[47] We suggest that the Valentinians have transferred similar considerations to the aeons above.

Moreover, the Valentinians believed that Saturn, the highest of the planets, symbolized the thirty aeons above, since it took thirty years to complete its cycle. Presumably they agreed, then, with the old schematic conception that Jupiter's cycle lasted twelve years, while that of the moon was one twelfth of a year (the year therefore lasted 360 days).[48] Modern astronomy had already indicated that the scheme was incorrect, but the Valentinians were concerned with the ideal rather than the real. In his attack on them, Irenaeus clearly shows both that their aeons were calendrical in origin and that there was something wrong with their calendar. He points out that the year has 365 days, not 360; that some months have thirty days, while others have either more or fewer.[49] He cannot criticize their twelve-month year, but he can complain about their identification of twelve aeons with twelve hours in a day. Actually, he says, the length of the day varies from nine hours to fifteen.[50]

We have said enough about the fours, the sevens, and the thirties of Gnostic thought to indicate, or at least to suggest, that they are all derived from the calendrical concern of apocalyptic Judaism. This kind of Jewish thought undoubtedly has Iranian, and perhaps Babylonian, roots. But for our purposes it is more important to insist on the significance of Judaism as the mediator of such notions.

How are we to explain the way in which this calendrical material was modified and transmuted in the Gnostic world? Presumably the process took place at a time when the importance of precise observance of calendrical law, or of any law, was being denied in Jewish circles. Already in the time of Philo there were allegorizers who found symbols in the Old Testament and believed that the symbols were so meaningful that literal observance of the law was unnecessary. Among gentile Christians too this view was prevalent. But it took the fall of Jerusalem to bring the old Jewish sacrificial system to an end. After the fall of Jerusalem it was fairly obvious, at least to Gnostics, that there was no point in observing a calendar, orthodox or heterodox. Yet since Jewish literature, both canonical and noncanonical, had been inspired by some god or other, it had to possess some meaning, presumably esoteric. It could be used to explain the workings of the celestial world, and indeed in the apocalypses such a meaning had already been indicated.

Once the failure of apocalyptic—to paraphrase Rowley's title, the irrelevance of apocalyptic—had revealed the unimportance of the earthly calendar, Gnostics turned to contemplate the eternal aeons from which conceptions of time were ultimately derived. The impetus for this turning was given by Hellenistic philosophy.

We see, therefore, that the heavenly world of the Gnostics is derived from several sources—a mixture of ideas chiefly Iranian and Greek, passed through the mixing-bowl of heterodox Judaism. The Dead Sea Scrolls show us the extent to which sectarian Judaism was being influenced by Iranian conceptions, and for the influence of Greek philosophy—especially Platonism—on Judaism we need look no farther than the voluminous works of Philo of Alexandria. For its picture of the heavenly world, Gnosticism relied on all these diverse elements, but its *immediate* sources were preeminently Jewish in form if not in substance.

The numbers of the celestial spirits are significant, but still more significant is the hostility of those who govern the world. Such hostility is to be found neither in Platonism, at least in orthodox Platonism, nor in Judaism, at least in orthodox Judaism. For such hostility we must turn once more to Zoroastrianism and to sectarian Judaism, and we must consider the conception of Satan as the enemy of God and man.

YAHWEH AS SATAN

We have already seen that many of the less lovable traits of Ialdabaoth are derived from his prototype Ahriman. But Ahriman also seems to have provided the prototype for the Jewish Satan. In the Old Testament Satan is, so to speak, de-Ahrimanized. He acts by God's permission; he is not an independent power. But in the extreme apocalyptic of the Dead Sea Scrolls we find more traces of Iranian dualism. The army of the Sons of Darkness is the army of the evil spirit Belial.[51] Indeed, "the sons of Israel are under the dominion of Belial." [52]

In the Dead Sea Scrolls there is not the faintest trace of the notion that "the God of Israel" is related to the evil spirit Belial. The two are irreconcilably opposed. We meet the prince of demons again in the New Testament, where Jesus is accused of casting out demons with the aid of

Beelzebul (Mark 3.22) and where he tells his disciples that
he has seen Satan fall from heaven like lightning (Luke
10.18). Some passages imply that Satan is the ruler of the
present age; thus in the temptation story he is evidently in
a position to offer Jesus "all the kingdoms of the world." [53]
He is opposed to the work of Jesus: both Luke (22.3) and
John (13.27) explain Judas' betrayal of Jesus as the work
of Satan.

In some parts of the New Testament we come closer to
Gnostic ideas. Thus, Paul speaks of Satan as "the god of
this age" (2 Cor. 4.4), and John calls him "the archon of
this world" (12.31; 14.30; 16.11). And at one point we are
surely on the very verge of the Gnostic idea. After "the
Jews" have told Jesus that God is their father (8.41), Jesus
replies that their father is not God but the devil (8.44). This
text could easily be understood as stating that Yahweh was
to be identified with Satan.[54] And it is our conviction that
such an identification was possible in circles of ex-Jews
after the fall of Jerusalem.

What can the origins of such a notion be? Actually, the
way toward it had been prepared within Judaism itself. In
the later books of the Old Testament we encounter God's
adversary Satan, and in a singular passage in 1 Chronicles
2.1 this adversary is substituted for God. The Chronicler
had read in 2 Samuel 24.1 that the angry Yahweh had inspired David to take a census and then had punished David
for doing so. He could not accept the story as it stood. He
therefore stated that Satan was the source of David's
inspiration. A pious modification, surely, but one which in

the hands of Gnostic exegetes could prove exceedingly dangerous.[55]

In the book of Jubilees, popular among the apocalyptists of Qumran, we find a similar attempt to free God from blame in various controversial stories of Israel's history. In Genesis 22.1 we read that it was God who tested Abraham by asking him to sacrifice Isaac. The story, however, speaks not only of God (Elohim) but also of "the angel of Yahweh." Jubilees 17.16 tells us that it was Mastema, prince of the angels hostile to man, who asked God to test Abraham. Again, in Exodus 4.24 we read that Yahweh tried to kill Moses; Jubilees 48.2–3 substitutes Mastema for Yahweh. Finally, Exodus 14.8 tells us that Yahweh hardened the heart of Pharaoh, while Jubilees 48.12 explains that his heart was hardened by Mastema, who had already helped the Egyptian magicians in their contendings with Moses (48.9).[56]

It is this kind of rewriting of scripture among apocalyptic enthusiasts which prepared the way for later Gnostic revisions of the Old Testament. We should also observe that the Gnostic theory of the inspiration of scripture by various angels is anticipated in Jubilees. When Moses wrote the story of creation, he did so under the inspiration of an angel of the Lord (2.1). Now Jubilees does *not* tell us that various angels inspired various parts of his work, but some such notion seems logically necessary to explain how Mastema and Yahweh got confused in the stories we have already mentioned. One way or another, interpolations must have slipped into the Old Testament.

If as Gnostic exegetes we look at the Old Testament, we obviously encounter a bewildering concatenation of divine names. As long as the Jewish community retained its center in the temple worship of the one God, authorized teachers could explain that all the divine names refer to him. But after the fall of the temple, unauthorized teachers could easily argue that various gods were to be found in the texts.[57]

After all, they could see that there is one creation story about the work of Elohim, and another about Yahweh Elohim; after this comes a narrative about the deeds of Yahweh. Later on, there is an extremely confusing story about the flood. In it some activities are assigned to Yahweh, others to Elohim. And in the patriarchal legends we read about Yahweh and about Elohim and about someone called "the angel of Yahweh" or "Yahweh the angel." The story of Jacob's blessing shows that Elohim is an angel too (Gen. 48.15–16). The beginning of Exodus adds further confusion. Yahweh tries to kill Moses (Ex. 4.24), and he says that while he appeared to the patriarchs as El-Shaddai, he was not known to them as Yahweh (Ex. 6.2–3).

Gnostic teachers could easily conclude that at least Yahweh and Elohim were angels, and that Yahweh was an unfriendly angel. By looking through some more of the Old Testament they could find the names of all seven hostile spirits. Relying on their own experience, on 1 Chronicles, and on apocalyptic literature, they could proceed to identify Yahweh with his adversary Satan.

Such a process, I believe, underlies John's statement about

the father of the Jews. It underlies the identification of
Ialdabaoth with Saclas in the Apocryphon of John.[58] And
it is reflected in the doctrine of the Cainites, who were
dealing primarily with problems of Old Testament
theology. They glorified Cain, the men of Sodom, and
Esau.[59] Undoubtedly they were, or had been, asking questions about the meaning of parts of the *Heilsgeschichte*.
Why did Yahweh prefer Abel's offering to that of Cain?
Why was he less merciful than Abraham, who asked him
to spare Sodom? [60] Why did he love Jacob and hate Esau?
Surely he must be a jealous, irrational god, inferior to some
supreme being.

One of the most singular features of Cainite doctrine is
their notion that the creator of heaven and earth, this god
inferior to Sophia, is to be called "womb" ($\dot{v}\sigma\tau\acute{\epsilon}\rho a$). How
can such an idea be explained? The background presumably
lies in exegesis of the Old Testament. There the Cainite
would notice that Yahweh will cry out like a travailing
woman (Isa. 42.14), and that he compares himself to a
woman who will not forget the child of her womb (Isa.
49.15). And when the Cainite looked for a proof text he
could find it in Exodus 34.6, where Yahweh says that his
name is "Yahweh, Yahweh, El רחום"; for it would be
simple enough to read רחום, "compassion," as רחם,
"womb." In this way a rabbinic method of exegesis could
be used by ex-Jews to create a thoroughly non-Jewish
theology.

Once more we should claim that this is the sort of development which takes place when men's apocalyptic hopes have failed and they are specifically seeking to find dualistic gnosis rather than prophecy in the Old Testament. All that the Cainite can hope for is escape from the created world.

ASCENT TO HEAVEN

Now if the heavenly world is populated by hostile spirits and there is a "blessed abode" somewhere above the heavens they occupy, the solution to the problem of human destiny is obviously to be found in an ascent to this dwelling place above. And since pictures of human destiny are always correlated with pictures of human nature, it is when man comes to be regarded as essentially soul or spirit that his goal can be regarded as a journey to the highest heaven. Among apocalyptic writers who look for intervention by God in the affairs of this world, we find belief in a future resurrection of dead bodies. In the later apocalyptic the bodies are regarded as quite new (2 Bar. 50–51). Among Gnostics, who do not expect such intervention, there is the expectation of an ascent of the divine spirit.

Such notions are obviously related to the Greco-Roman idea of celestial immortality,[61] and the "heavenly journey of the soul" is also found in Iranian and specifically Mithraic sources.[62] But the full flowering of the idea is present in such Jewish books as the Testament of Levi, 2 Enoch, and 2 Baruch,[63] and it would seem that from them it passed into

Christian and Gnostic teaching. According to Josephus it
was also to be found among the Essenes.[64] We meet it in
the Gospel of John, as we shall see.

In order to reach the highest heaven the spirit must pass
through the lower heavens, governed by "archons." This
term means simply "rulers," but in Gnostic thought it
comes to have a technical significance. Its meaning in relation to the planets is already set forth by Philo, who tells
us that sun, moon, and stars are "archons, not independent
but subordinate to the one Father of all." [65] Apocalyptic
and Gnostic speculation, however, soon seized on the
mysterious mentions of the archons in the book of Psalms,
where "archons" are clearly hostile to God.

The archons came together against the Lord [Ps. 2.2].
The Lord will destroy the plans of the archons [32(33).10].
Annihilation was poured forth on the archons [106(107).40].
The archons persecuted me to no avail [118(119).161].
Put not your trust in archons [145(146).3].

And Psalm 81 (82) would make the point especially clear.

> They did not know or understand,
> They walk in darkness,
> All the foundations of the earth will be shaken.
> I said, You are gods,
> And all sons of the Most High;
> But you die like men,
> And fall like one of the archons.

With these passages in mind, an apocalyptic or Gnostic
exegete could hardly fail to be impressed by Psalm
23(24).7–9.

> Lift up the gates, ye archons,
> And be lifted up, ye eternal gates,
> And the king of glory will enter in.

Who are the archons? Who is the king of glory? The answer to this question is provided once one has realized that the archons are the planetary spirits.

The planetary spirits do not need to be regarded as hostile except in a Gnostic environment. The non-Gnostic Justin is quite willing to say that "the archons were set in the heavens by God, to open the gates of the heavens." When Christ ascended they did not recognize him, since he was "without form" (Isa. 53.2), so they asked who the king of glory was and the Holy Spirit told them he was Christ.[66] On the other hand, in Christian writings closer to Gnosticism Christ is transformed as he descends through the spheres of the archons so that they will not recognize him.[67] And in Gnostic circles the same story is told of Simon Magus and of the Christ-power which descended upon Jesus.[68]

In the Gnostic view these descents took place so that the way of ascent could be made plain. As Simon or the Christ-power descended, so you too may ascend. There are differences within the Gnostic systems. We do not hear of a story of Simon's ascension, while we do hear that the Christ-power returned to its home in the highest heaven above. But the main point is clear. You must know the archons of the various heavens, so that you can address them by name. And you must know magical passwords which will give you further control over them.

In the Ascension of Isaiah (10.24–29) we read that when
Jesus descended through the heavens he gave passwords to
the three lowest gatekeepers, but we are not told what the
passwords were. On the other hand, both Irenaeus and
Origen are delighted to be able to reveal the passwords
which Gnostics intended to employ.[69] The Marcosians—
magic-minded Valentinians—had invocations which would
make their "inner man" incomprehensible and invisible to
the principalities and powers; these invocations emphasized
the celestial origin of the initiate and made the angels of the
Demiurge run away.[70] The Ophites took with them not
only formulas but also symbols with pictures engraved on
them, presumably something like the "Gnostic gems"
preserved in museums today.

Both Marcosians and Ophites, like Jesus himself, thus
possessed formulas by means of which they could overcome the hostile planetary powers, and ascend to the
highest heaven. Instead of awaiting the coming of God's
kingdom on earth, like the apocalyptic enthusiasts of
earlier times, they looked only for escape from earth and
from its creators. To be sure, they did not expect to escape
during the life-term to which they had been sentenced.
But escape by dying was sure to come.

It was sure to come because the way had been shown
them by the redeemer, but not by the redeemer alone. In
Jewish apocalyptic writings we already read of those who
have visited heaven. Such a notion is found in the Testament of Levi, in the Enoch literature, and in the apocalypses of Abraham and Moses and others. All these Old

Testament heroes visited heaven and then reported the revelations given them there. And it was quite obvious from reading Genesis that before their expulsion both Adam and Eve had been in paradise, often located in one of the heavens above. If the end was to be like the beginning, it was certain that the end was to be sought above.

In Christian and Jewish circles we hear of more recent ascensions. The apostle Paul tells us about a man (presumably himself) who "whether in the body or apart from the body" visited the third heaven and paradise and there heard "ineffable words" (2 Cor. 12.2–4). Paul's doubts about his physical ascension, and the ineffability of the words he heard, suggest that we are confronted with some kind of mystical experience. Such experience was not confined to him alone. In the second century it was said that four rabbis had "entered the garden"—paradise, the heavenly garden of Eden. For three of them the effect was unfortunate. One went mad; another died; a third took up magic. Only Akiba "entered in peace and came out in peace." [71] And like him, the author of the Gospel of Truth once "sojourned in the place of Rest." [72] The difference between the ordinary Jewish or Christian view and that of the Gnostic is this: neither Paul nor Akiba was transformed by the experience of ascension. Valentinus, however, came to be "in true and eternal life" because of his sojourning.[73]

None of the ascensions we have been mentioning are ascensions of a redeemer, and thus far we have mentioned no redeemer who descended from heaven in order to show men the way upward. Such redeemers are hard to find.

Indeed, in the early centuries of our era we can discover
only three: Jesus, Simon Magus, and Menander. It is
extraordinarily difficult to believe that the stories of Simon
and Menander are not based on the story of Jesus. And we
must therefore attempt to consider how it came about that
Jesus was said to have descended from heaven.

DESCENT FROM HEAVEN

It is easier to say that some early Christians believed that
Jesus had come down from heaven than to explain why
they so believed. To be sure, Paul tells us that in the future
Jesus will come down (1 Thess. 4.16; see also Phil. 3.20),
but such a descent is presumably based on belief in his
resurrection and exaltation. On the other hand, in Ephesians
4.8–10 we find exegesis of Psalm 68.18, where the word
"ascended" is taken to imply that Jesus had also "descended." But this exegesis can hardly be the source of the
belief; more probably it reflects a prior belief. A similar
observation can be made with regard to John 3.13: "no one
has ascended into heaven but he who descended from
heaven, the Son of Man." John knows that the Son of Man
descended; but how does he know?

Two interwoven lines of investigation may be suggested.
In the Old Testament we read of the sacred Name of God
which has "tabernacled" in the temple (Jer. 7.12) or will
"tabernacle" there (Ezek. 43.7) or will "tabernacle" in the
midst of the people (Ps. Sol. 7.5). Again, we read of the
Wisdom of God which "came forth from the mouth of the

Most High" (Sirach 24.3), tabernacled in Jacob, and was the inheritance of Israel (24.8).[74] According to 1 Enoch 42.2 she "went out to dwell among the children of men." And in the book of Wisdom (7.27), "in every generation she passes into holy souls." Both the Name of God and the Wisdom of God can be viewed as equivalent to his Shekinah, his presence as revealed to men, and thus it becomes significant that at least according to some rabbis the Shekinah does descend to earth. Odeberg[75] cites a rabbinic list of ten such descents recorded in the Old Testament.

These passages are important because they show how one who in Paul's belief was the Image of God (see Wisdom 7, 26) and the Wisdom of God could descend from heaven, and how John could speak of the pre-existent Word of God as becoming flesh and "tabernacling" among men (John 1.14). From this beginning in Jewish thought about the Name and the Wisdom of God came the Christian belief in the descent of Christ from heaven. Teaching about the Name is conspicuous in early Christian prayers, not only in the high-priestly prayer of John 17 but also in 1 Clement 59.3 ("thy Name, first-born of all creation") and Didache 10.2 ("thy holy Name, which thou didst tabernacle in our hearts") and 10.3 ("thou didst create all things for the sake of thy Name"). According to Hermas (Sim. ix.14.5), "the Name of the Son of God is great and incomprehensible and bears the whole world." Its utterance founded the Church (Vis. iii.3.5).

From belief in the descent of God's Name, Wisdom, and Shekinah came belief in the descent of the Son of Man, for in pre-Christian Jewish literature, as J. A. T. Robinson has pointed out, there is no notion that the, or a, Messiah or Son of Man will descend from heaven.[76] Again, were one to seek the origin of Paul's idea of the descent of a Second Adam in the fall of the first, one would have to remember that while he draws analogies between the two in 1 Corinthians 15.45–49, he points out in Romans 5 that the differences are more important than the resemblances (see Rom. 5.15–16). If the paradise from which Adam came is located in the third heaven (2 Cor. 12.2–3), Adam fell, while Christ descended.

Similarly in Philippians 2.6–11 a contrast is drawn between Christ and Adam. Adam wanted to "grasp" equality with God; in Eden the serpent had told Adam and Eve that they would be "like Elohim" (Gen. 3.5) and God himself had not wanted them to grasp the fruit of the tree of life (3.22). Christ, on the other hand, "emptied himself" and exchanged his divine "form" (as the Image of God) for that of a slave; because of his obedience and humility God gave him "the Name above every name." Here the conception of the descent of the Name is not developed; instead, we are in a different atmosphere, where the Name is a post-resurrection gift rather than a pre-incarnation possession. Yet we cannot be sure that original possession is excluded, since in 2 Corinthians 8.9 Paul says of Christ that "though he was rich, yet for your sake he became poor."

In any event, the Christian conception of the descent of Christ is developed out of previous Jewish teaching, not about the, or a, Messiah, whose descent from heaven is never mentioned, but about God's Wisdom and his Name and his presence among men. And there is no reason to suppose that it reflects an earlier Gnostic doctrine about the descent of a redeemer, especially since there is no evidence that such a doctrine existed.

3

SIMON MAGUS AND HELEN, HIS THOUGHT

ANY ACCOUNT of the development of Gnosticism has to be concerned with the elusive person and doctrine of Simon Magus, since such Christian writers as Justin, Hegesippus, Irenaeus, and the author of the Acts of the Apostles regard him as the earliest Gnostic. He has long appealed to the imagination of the Western World. Prominent in the Clementine romances, he was later transformed into the Doctor Faustus of medieval legend,[1] and from his name comes the word *simony*. The poet Apollinaire, renouncing traditional culture in 1913, compared the recent cross-channel flight of Blériot with the flight Simon was said to have made over the city of Rome,[2] though he did not mention the fact that in the Christian story Simon was brought down by the prayer of the apostle Peter.

According to Irenaeus, Simon taught that he had "appeared among the Jews as Son, descended in Samaria as Father, and came among the other nations as Holy Spirit."[3] We shall later discuss the probable Christian origin of this doctrine. Here, however, we wish simply to use the statement symbolically to indicate that in the documents we

possess there are three Simons, not just one. There is the
Simon of the book of Acts; there is the Simon of Justin
and Irenaeus; and there is the Simon of the pseudo-Clementine *Homilies* and *Recognitions*. And it is a real question
whether or not these three are one.

THE SIMON OF ACTS

The oldest account of Simon occurs in the book of Acts,[4]
where we read that he was converted by the evangelist
Philip; "he believed and was baptized." But he had not received the Holy Spirit, which was given only by the im-
position of the apostles' hands, and when Peter and John
came to Samaria from Jerusalem he offered them money
for the privilege of transmitting it. Peter vehemently rejected his offer. The scene closes with Simon's request to
the apostles to pray for him. From this little story we learn
that Simon was a magician, that he "said he was some great
one," and that his admirers called him "the great Power
of God." We do not learn what happened to him afterwards.

The first problem which arises in relation to this account
has to do with the purpose of the author of Acts. Is he
simply relating what he knows about early Christianity in
Samaria? Is his story inconclusive because he lacks further
information? Or is he telling his story, like others, under
the spell of his own theories of the way early Christianity
should have developed? Is he trying to show, for example,
that all missionary activity was under the control of the

Jerusalem church, and that Jerusalem apostles were needed in order to expose an insincere magician? Does he have the erroneous notion that there was no heresy until the end of the apostolic age, and therefore refrains from mentioning Simon's Gnostic doctrine? [5] To ask such questions is easier than to answer them. I should like to suggest the possibility that Luke is simply telling what he thinks happened. Is it not equally likely that at one stage in his career a Samaritan magician recognized a religious power greater than his own?

But we are still left with a second problem, arising out of the mysterious title which Samaritans gave Simon, "the great Power of God." What can it mean? Two parallels often cited [6] seem to point in the same direction. One is an acclamation of the god Mēn, found in an Asia Minor inscription, which probably reads: "One [is] god in the heavens; great [is] the heavenly Mēn; great [is] the power of the immortal god." [7] The other occurs in a magical papyrus, where the magician invokes "thee, the greatest power, set in heaven by the Lord God." It is possible that in performing his magic Simon too invoked such a god or such a power, and that a successful performance was followed by the identification of the power with Simon himself. In any event, from Acts we learn nothing about Simon as a Gnostic teacher or redeemer, and we hear nothing about his being accompanied by the Helen of whom the Church Fathers made so much. Had the author of Acts known of her, it seems unlikely that he would have remained silent about her.

Acts does say that Simon won a great many adherents

among the Samaritans (indeed, "all from small to great"),
and we may wonder what, if anything, his mission had to
do with the "prophet" who in A.D. 36 gathered a throng
to ascend Mount Gerizim to find the sacred vessels, the
loss of which, hundreds of years earlier, had inaugurated
the period of God's disfavor. It was Pontius Pilate who had
many of the prophet's followers put to death, while the
vessels were not recovered.[8] Could it be that Simon was
more closely related to the Samaritan religion than Luke,
who regards Samaria as a Christian mission field, wants to
admit? Could it be that he was regarded as the *Ta'eb* or
"restorer" of the Samaritans? These questions cannot be
answered on the grounds of the evidence we now have,
but it is at least possible that Simon's gospel was eschatological as well as magical, and that Gnostic reinterpretation arose out of the failure of his mission.

THE SIMON OF JUSTIN

To find out anything about Gnostic Simonianism we have
to go on to Justin, a Samaritan by birth, who wrote his
first apology at Rome about 150. It is not evident that
Justin's Samaritan origin means that his information comes
from Samaria. Certainly, some of it comes from Rome, for
he tells us that under Claudius the Senate and the Roman
people (SPQR) were so strongly influenced by Simon's
magic that on Tiber Island they erected a statue to him
with the inscription SIMONI DEO SANCTO.[9] Presumably Justin
was looking at, or hearing about, the inscription as viewed

through eyes of Simonian faith, for an inscription actually found on the island in 1574 reads: SEMONI SANCO DEO FIDIO —a dedication to a god of oaths, heaven, thunder, and lightning.[10] It may have been related to a shrine of Jupiter,[11] and since Simonians were accustomed to identify Simon with this god, they thus had two points of departure.[12] Now since this much of Justin's information is Roman, we may well wonder whether the rest of it does not come from Roman Simonians too.

"Nearly all the Samaritans," he says (possibly relying on Acts 8.9–10), "and a few among other peoples, acknowledge and worship Simon as the First God, and they say that a certain Helen, who accompanied him at that time but was formerly a prostitute (ἐπὶ στέγους), was the First Thought which he brought into existence." [13] Several inferences can be drawn from these remarks. If the First God had a First Thought, presumably the existing universe originated through her. And if the First Thought was once a prostitute, somehow or other she must have been degraded so that the First God had to come down to rescue her. In other words, in what Justin's Simonian informants told him they were alluding to their whole myth of creation, fall, and redemption.

Needless to say, Justin is not convinced that Simon was the First God. Indeed, he tells us that he really came not from heaven but from a Samaritan village named Gitta. Thus, he attacks him on grounds not unlike those used by Jesus' opponents in the Gospel of John when they criticize his heavenly origin because he came from Galilee.[14] We may suppose that Simon did come from Gitta, just as Jesus did come from Nazareth.

One more bit of Simonian doctrine may be reflected in another passage in Justin's work. There we read that demons call Korê the daughter of Zeus and erect her image at springs and call Athena the daughter of Zeus, his First Thought.[15] This statement may be no more than a bit of Hellenistic *Religionsgeschichte*. But the expression "First Thought" seems to be Simonian rather than Greco-Roman. At Samaria was worshiped the goddess Helen, whose statue has been found with attributes of Korê,[16] while from Irenaeus we know that Simonians worshiped their Helen as Athena. Therefore, Justin may be referring to Simonian teaching at this point.

From what Justin tells us we can certainly infer that in his time Simonian doctrine, at least at Rome, was fully developed to a fair degree. It is uncertain whether Simonians or their opponents said that Simon came from Gitta, but the Simonians themselves certainly held that he had come to Rome. Their faith could be confirmed by archaeology. On the other hand, we have absolutely no evidence to show that their myth about the First God and his First Thought goes back to a time before the beginning of the second century. In other words, while Justin apparently identifies the Simonian Simon with the magician of Acts, it is by no means certain that we should follow his example.

SOPHIA'S FALL AND REDEMPTION

The next stage in the development of Simonian doctrine, or at least of what we know about Simonian doctrine, is found in an account given by Irenaeus about 180. In this account we find a much fuller description of the creation, the fall of the First Thought, and the saving work of Simon.[17] We learn that Helen came from Tyre, and that Simon called her not only First Thought of his mind but also Mother of All. We learn that Simon was worshiped as Zeus, Helen as Athena. There is a semipoetic structure in the story of her early life which reminds us of the prologue to the Gospel of John.[18]

In the beginning the Father planned to create angels and arch-
    angels.
His Thought leaped forth from him, knowing her Father's will;
She descended to the lower regions.
She generated angels and powers, by whom this world was
    made.
But after she generated them, she was held captive by them,
Because of jealousy;
For they were unwilling to be thought the offspring of any
    other.
The Father himself was absolutely unknown to them;
But his Thought was held captive by them—
The powers emitted by her, and the angels—
She suffered every disgrace from them,
So that she could not return to her Father,
But was even imprisoned in a human body,

And through all ages passed as from vessel to vessel,
Into one female body after another.

This structure, again as in the Johannine prologue, is interrupted by a prose comment which links the myth with history.[19] "The Thought was in that Helen on whose account the Trojan War was undertaken; for this reason, when Stesichorus slandered her in his poems he was deprived of his sight, but when he later repented and wrote the *Palinodes* in which he gave praise to her, he saw again." [20] This represents an attempt by the Simonians to point to a specific example of the presence of the Thought in historical events. Then the poetic myth continues.

She passed from body to body,
Always suffering disgrace from it;
Last of all [or, "at the end of these days" (Heb. 1.2)]
She was manifest in a prostitute;
This is the lost sheep [Luke 15.6].
For her sake He came,
To free her from her bonds,[21]
And to offer men salvation
Through their recognition of him [cf. Luke 1.71, 77].
For when the angels misgoverned the world,
Since each of them desired the primacy,
He came for the restoration of all things,
Transformed and made like the principalities and powers.[22]
With men he seemed a man, though not a man;
He seemed to suffer in Judaea,
Though he did not suffer.

Here, then, is an authentic Ennoialogical (or Helenalogical) and Simonological hymn or poem, presumably used by

Simonians at Rome or elsewhere in the middle of the second
century. It consists of three parts, the first dealing with the
generation and fall of Sophia-Ennoia, the second with her
early life on earth, and the third with her rescue by Simon.

Her relation to the Trojan War deserves some attention,
for it represents a significant attempt by the Simonians,
like other Gnostics in the second and third centuries, to
find links between themselves and Hellenistic culture. The
way had been prepared for them, it should be added, both
by Jewish and by Samaritan writers in the Hellenistic age.[23]
Direct quotations provided by Epiphanius in the fourth
century seem to be derived from much earlier Simonian
material.[24]

She who at that time was with the Greeks and Trojans was
the same who dwelt above before creation, and after creation
had made copies through the invisible powers. She is the one
who now is with me; for her sake I descended. She waited
for my coming; for she is the Thought called Helen in Homer.
For this reason Homer has to describe her as having stood on
the tower and signaling with a torch to the Greeks the plot
against the Phrygians. Through its shining, as I said, he signified
the display of the light from above. . . . As the Phrygians by
dragging in the wooden horse ignorantly brought on their own
destruction, so the gentiles, i.e. men apart from my gnosis,
produce perdition for themselves.

Hippolytus describes her activities a little more fully.[25]

Ever dwelling in women, she was disturbing the powers in the
world because of her insurpassable beauty; for this reason the
Trojan War took place on her account. For in the Helen who
lived at that time dwelt the Thought, and so, when all the

powers were claiming her, discord and war arose among those nations where she appeared.

Then follows the story about Stesichorus, who first reviled her but then realized that Helen had not really been in Troy at all. Instead, a "phantom" (εἴδωλον) of her had been there.

Several inferences can be drawn from this story about Helen of Troy. First, the Simonians were enthusiastic about Homer and regarded him as inspired, presumably by Simon's Thought. Second, they knew something about Homeric exegesis; they were acquainted with the ideas of Stesichorus and other allegorizers. But, third, their reach exceeded their grasp. It is not Homer who says that Helen showed the way to the Greeks, but later retellers of the story, such as Virgil and Tryphiodorus.[26] And the theory of Stesichorus does not really fit Simonian doctrine. In his view the real Helen was not at Troy but with Menelaus in Egypt.[27]

We should conclude, therefore, that the story about Simon's Thought as Helen of Troy represents window dressing by Simonians anxious to minimize the distance between their founder and themselves. Samaritan worship of the goddess Helen may have played some part in this work. It recalls the efforts of early Christian apologists to show that their religion was anticipated by the best that had been thought and said among the Greeks. The difference in the results may well be related to the difference between Simon and Jesus.

Now, turning back to the first part of the Simonian story,

we note once more that in some respects it resembles the
prologue to the Fourth Gospel. Commentators have often
pointed out how much the prologue itself seems to owe
to earlier descriptions of the Jewish Sophia of God. (We
shall later return to this subject, in Chapter 6.) And it is
quite possible that both Christians and Simonians have relied upon similar sources. There are two striking differences, however. Simon's Sophia becomes incarnate as a
result of the envy of angels; the Logos becomes incarnate
"for us men and for our salvation." And Simon's Sophia
suffers because she is in the flesh, while the flesh of Jesus is
part of God's plan. We can understand the Christian story
as an interpretation of the life of Jesus—pre-existent Word
and Wisdom of God. But how are we to explain the creative activity and the fall of Simon's Sophia?

First, we must consider the origins of Simon's First
Thought as such. The most obvious parallels to a god's
First Thought are provided in Hellenistic philosophy and
rhetoric and in the Jewish Wisdom literature. Allegorizers
of mythology were accustomed to explain the old story
about Athena's birth from the top of Zeus's head as the
production of his Forethought or Intelligence or Wisdom,
and speculation about her origin may have gone on on Semitic soil; Ralph Marcus claimed that an etymological explanation of her name as "I came from myself" was possible only on the basis of Aramaic.[28] A Jewish counterpart
of such speculation is provided in the Wisdom literature,
where we meet the personified Wisdom of God. She was
God's helper in the work of creation (Prov. 8.22–31); she

prepared a dwelling for herself and hewed out seven mysterious pillars (9.1), which may be planets or planetary
spirits. More than that, Philo calls her the daughter of God,
the bride of God, and the Mother of All.[29] Presumably it
was by developing speculations like these that the Simonians
created their story of the First Thought.

But we still have nothing to explain how she fell and
became a captive of the angels. The explanation most
widely held today is provided by looking in the vicinity of
Tyre, the city where Simon met Helen. Bousset suggested
that a clue may be given by the fourth-century Christian
writer Epiphanius, who said that the goddess Isis was once
a prostitute in Tyre.[30] The trouble with this clue is that
Epiphanius may simply be drawing on the rich resources
of his imagination; but his mention of Isis may well lead
us in the direction of some Semitic love goddess, since we
know that she was sometimes identified with both Astarte
and Aphrodite, and that Astarte was the principal goddess
of Tyre.[31] A parallel to the Simonian story is provided by
a story current in the Near East for at least a thousand
years, from the time it was told of the Sumerian queen of
heaven, Inanna, in the first half of the second millennium
B.C., until the time it was told of the Akkadian queen of
heaven, Ishtar, in the seventh century.[32]

The story of Inanna tells how she abandoned heaven,
abandoned earth, and descended to the nether world. In
each of seven Sumerian cities she abandoned her temples.
When she reached the seven gates of the nether world she
was met by the gatekeeper of Ereshkigal, goddess of the

nether world, and he opened them for her one by one. At the first gate he removed her crown, at the second her measuring rod, at the third her lapis lazuli necklace, at the fourth the sparkling stones from her breast, at the fifth her gold ring, at the sixth her breastplate, and at the seventh the remainder of her clothing. In the presence of Ereshkigal, seven judges pronounced judgment upon her. She became a corpse and was hung from a stake, for three days and nights. Finally, the great father Enki missed the presence of "the queen of all the lands," "the hierodule of heaven," and ordered the food and water of life sprinkled on Inanna's corpse. She rose and ascended from the nether world to occupy new temples and to forgive their tutelary deities for occupying them, since they belonged to her.

Approximately the same story is told of Ishtar in a Babylonian magical text which was to be used as an incantation for raising one's sister from the dead.[33] Ishtar goes down to the "land of no return," to the "house of darkness." At seven gates she is stripped naked, and Ereshkigal instructs her vizier to release against her the sixty miseries, miseries in eyes, sides, feet, and head, in her whole body. The supreme god Ea, observing that human and animal sexual activity has stopped, creates a eunuch who descends to recover Ishtar. Ishtar is sprinkled with the water of life and, reclothed, ascends to earth.

Now since this text comes from the seventh century B.C., we may well wonder how it can be used to illustrate a doctrine of the first century of the Christian era. Here two answers can be suggested. In the first place, the myth of Korê's descent into the underworld is first known to us from the "Homeric Hymn to Demeter," roughly contemporary with the magical text or a little later than it. From later Greek literature we know that the story continued to be told and that it was related to the Eleusinian mysteries and therefore became all the more popular. So we may argue that lack of knowledge about the later transmission of Babylonian myths does *not* imply that they were *not* transmitted, especially at shrines. In Plutarch's treatise on Isis there is much material which can be illustrated from ancient Egyptian sources. In the second place, we know that in Phoenicia early in the second century A.D. there was a considerable interest in ancient Phoenician mythology. The Greek grammarian Philo of Byblos collected materials from earlier writings, and their reliability was at least partly confirmed by the discovery, between 1929 and 1933, of Ugaritic tablets from the fourteenth century B.C. It was therefore perfectly possible for ancient myths to be preserved and known.

It was also possible for stories to be transferred from one goddess to another. We have already seen that what was told of Inanna came to be told of Ishtar. But if we look for known combinations which can be related to the story of Simon's Thought, we may take as a starting point the remark of A. D. Nock that "Isis was a strong central point for equations." Thus, the Egyptian priest Manetho tells us that "people often call Isis Athena," [34] and we know that Simonians worshiped Helen as Athena. Manetho also says that Isis is to be identified with the moon,[35] and some

Simonians called Helen *Luna*. Both Plutarch and Apuleius tell us that Isis can be identified with Persephone (Korê),[36] and we have found a trace of such an identification in Justin.

Moreover, Isis was identified with Syrian and Babylonian goddesses. An Oxyrhynchus papyrus of the second century (XI, 1380) tells us that Isis is "in Susa, Nania; in Phoenicia, the Syrian goddess; in Sidon, Astarte." And another papyrus [37] shows that Isis Nanaia was worshiped in Egypt. Who is Nania? She is the old Babylonian goddess Inanna, the one who descended to the lower world and was mistreated at its seven gates.

Finally, Isis also had philosophical and cosmological significance. Plutarch tells us that she was sometimes called Sophia,[38] and the Christian apologist Athenagoras informs us that as Athena was called Forethought ($\phi\rho\acute{o}\nu\eta\sigma\iota\varsigma$) so Isis was called $\phi\acute{v}\sigma\iota\varsigma$ $\alpha\grave{\iota}\hat{\omega}\nu o\varsigma$, "from which all grew and through which all exist." [39]

These parallels do not prove that the Simonians made use of just these combinations of ideas; they do show that such combinations were possible, and they indicate something of the speculative background in which they were made.

These are some of the ingredients which may have gone into the Simonian portrait of Helen: something about the Wisdom of God, combined with the old story of the degradation of Ishtar and her experiences in the underworld.[40] (In true Gnostic fashion Simonians found hell on earth.) But I must confess that I am not entirely satisfied with this analysis. Is it not possible to find the First Thought in the Old Testament? It might be suggested that we should fol-

low another line of investigation. Among the rabbis it was
sometimes held that it was Israel for whom and through
whom God effected the work of creation,[41] and Israel could
thus be identified with God's pre-existent Wisdom. From
the Old Testament one could infer that Israel suffered
much not only from the nations but from the angels who
governed the nations. And finally one could find a prototype for Simon in the marriage of Hosea to a prostitute,
symbolic of God's relation with his people Israel. Just so,
Simon found Helen as a prostitute in Tyre. Like Wisdom
in Proverbs 8.2–4, she was doubtless inviting men to herself
on heights, at crossroads, at city gates. Simonian theologians
would recognize that Simon was acting a parable of his
relation to Israel, or to a remnant of Israel. They would
further correlate his action with the search for the lost
sheep of Luke 15.6, or more explicitly with Matthew
15.24: "I was sent only to the lost sheep of the house of
Israel."

With this conception in mind one could understand how
freedom was to be achieved by rejecting conventional morality; for the message of Hosea could be interpreted in this
way, especially in the light of Ephesians,[42] which as we shall
see the Simonians read.

SIMON AND JESUS

Now we must go on to ask what we learn of Simon in the
soteriological section of the Simonian hymn. First we learn
that he came for the sake of the lost sheep, presumably the

lost sheep of the parable in Luke 15.6. In other words, like (or as) the Son of Man, he "came to seek and to save that which was lost" (Luke 19.10). Presumably the Simonians are simply interpreting the story of Jesus, the good shepherd, in relation to Helen. Parallels to the offering of salvation through recognition are also to be found in the Gospel of Luke (1.71, 77).

But this is not the only explanation of Simon's advent. It is also stated that the angels were misgoverning the world, since each of them desired the primacy. Such a doctrine is not necessarily Gnostic; we find it also in a fragment from the second-century Jewish Christian Papias.[43] And when we hear that Simon came for "the restoration of all things," this statement is both astrological—referring to the planets' return to their original positions—and Christian (Acts 3.21).

The idea that Simon was "transformed and made like the principalities and powers," no doubt so that they would not recognize him, is found in relation to Jesus in all the other second-century literature we know.[44] And the statement that "he seemed to be a man" and "seemed to suffer in Judaea" is obviously an interpretation of the life and death of Jesus. Who is being described in this soteriological fragment? Is it Simon, whose name is never mentioned? Or is it Simon as Jesus, Simon as Son? It would seem that all this part of the Simonian hymn is simply taken over, without much alteration, if any, from a Christian myth about Jesus. Confirmation of this conclusion is provided by another statement Irenaeus makes about Simon. He was the Highest Power, the Father above all, but he was willing to be called by any name men might use. He "appeared among the Jews as Son, descended in Samaria as Father, and came among the other nations as Holy Spirit." It is almost beyond doubt that this statement is based on the Christian baptismal formula of the late first century which we find at the end of the Gospel of Matthew (28.19): "baptizing them into the name of the Father and of the Son and of the Holy Spirit." Simonians have rearranged the sequence of names because of their own *Heilsgeschichte*. First came Jesus, the Son; then came Simon, the Father; now Simon is present among all nations as the Holy Spirit.[45] This is clear evidence for Simonian borrowing from Christianity.

If the search for the lost sheep is Christian, and the coming of Simon through the spheres and his revelation of himself as Son and Father and Holy Spirit is Christian, we are not left with much which could be considered authentically Simon's. What we have is the syncretistic effort of a Samaritan magician or his followers to explain the meaning of his relation to a woman he found in Tyre. He saved her. He can save you too, say the Simonians, if you have faith in him and in Helen.

But what does Simon save us from? The Christians say that Jesus saves from sin, from the law, from principalities and powers, from death. But we Simonians say the same thing in a different way—though our sources do not mention Simon's saving us from death. Simon gives us a this-worldly salvation. And if we ask how this salvation is effected, we learn that it comes through recognition of Simon

and Helen, and through rejection of conventional morality.
The angels who made the world wanted to enslave men,
just as they had enslaved Helen. They therefore gave commandments such as those found in the law used by Jews
and Samaritans alike. We, who have "set our hope" on
Simon and Helen, are "saved by his grace, not by just
works" (a quotation from Ephesians 2.8–9), and we are
therefore free to do what we wish. Once more, it is hard
to believe that this doctrine is not based on Christian theology, especially when we know that the apostle Paul struggled to define his own understanding of grace and presumably did not obtain it ready-made from the Simonians.
Freedom from slavery to law-giving angels may well be
derived from his epistle to the Galatians (3.19: see also
4.1–10).

At this point we must face one more difficult problem.
Does all this information really refer to the Simonians or
does it come from Ebionites who used the figure of Simon
in order to attack Paul? Strange though it may seem, such
use is actually found in the *Clementine Homilies* and *Recognitions* and in their sources, which go back to the second
century.[46] And we must regretfully add that Irenaeus seems
to be acquainted with something like these sources when
he tells us that, after the incident described in Acts, Simon
"eagerly proceeded to contend with the apostles." [47] In
other words, are parts of his account of Simonianism simply
derived from Ebionite attacks on Paul? No certainty is
attainable, but to me it appears more likely that the Simonians actually were radical Paulinists, at least in some measure,

and that at a later point the Ebionites recognized this fact and attacked Paul through Simon. I should hold that what Irenaeus says is Simonian is Simonian.

In other words, to a very considerable extent Western Simonianism is simply a parasitic growth upon early Christianity. It is far more syncretistic than early Christianity was, partly because it arose on non-Jewish soil. But its roots seem to lie in Judaism and Christianity. It is difficult to explain the story of Helen's decline and fall apart from a a combination of Jewish Sophia with Tyrian Ishtar, or perhaps with Israel. It is impossible to explain the advent of Simon apart from Christian teaching about Jesus. And the meaning of the salvation provided by Simon is described in language borrowed from some, at least, of the Pauline Epistles.[48]

Chronological considerations may help us here. Around 150 there were still disciples of Menander who thought they were immortal; Justin says so.[49] Now Justin also says that Menander was the disciple of Simon, and Justin, himself a Samaritan in origin, may well have known what he was talking about. Even allowing for lots of longevity, it seems hard to place Menander's discipleship before 70. Is it not likely, then, that Simonian Gnosticism arose chiefly after the destruction of the temple, even though Simon the Samaritan magician was at work a generation earlier? Admittedly we cannot trace the precise development of Simonian doctrines and say which are early and which are late. But it seems likely to me that as a system Simonianism is a late first-century creation.

EASTERN SIMONIANISM

Thus far we have been dealing with the Simonian gnosis which spread from Samaria to Rome and is discussed by writers who, whatever their origins were, attacked Simonianism in its Roman form. The same observation can be made with regard to the "Great Declaration" partly reproduced by Hippolytus.[50] This document seems to have been influenced by Valentinian doctrine, and it represents Simonianism in semiphilosophical dress. What the Roman versions of Simonian doctrine show is that Simonianism, in the West borrowed from its rival Christianity and that like Christianity it was capable of doctrinal development. These versions do not really tell us anything about Simonian origins.

Fortunately, we are not limited to analysis of Western Simonianism but possess documents which, in spite of their obscurity, provide us with an alternative. These are the pseudo-Clementine *Homilies* and *Recognitions*, which in their present form come from the fourth century but reflect Simonian doctrine not only different from but earlier than the records of Roman Christians.

In the Clementine versions we read that John the Baptist had thirty disciples, corresponding to the days of the lunar month, or more accurately 29½, since one was a woman named Helen or Selene. After John's death, a certain Dositheus became chief of the sect. Later the magician Simon, son of Antonius and Rachel, became one of the thirty and finally replaced Dositheus as "the standing one" (ὁ ἑστώς).

Who was Dositheus? He is mentioned along with Simon as a Jewish Christian or Samaritan heretic, and Origen gives an example of his rigorous interpretation of the law. Some of Dositheus' disciples held that he had not really died.[51] As late as the sixth century there were controversies among the Samaritans as to whether the "prophet like Moses" was Joshua or Dositheus.[52] And the convergent testimony of Epiphanius and an Arabic chronicle of the fourteenth century[53] suggest that the Dositheans were adherents of a rigorist sect which arose in Maccabean times, rejecting the ordinary dates for festivals and insisting upon a lunar month of thirty days, refusing to speak of Yahweh or Adonai and substituting the name Elohim, and apparently making much use of ritual washings. It is natural to compare this sect with the Qumran community, especially since in one of the Arabic accounts we read that it was gathered in the vicinity of Jerusalem, and that at one point it was persecuted by the Jewish high priest.

From this evidence, heterogenous though it is, we should conclude that the Dositheans were somehow related to the Dead Sea community. Perhaps they could be called schismatic schismatics, combining Jewish with Samaritan notions as the Dead Sea people combined them, but giving more weight to Samaritan influence.

If this can be regarded as the environment out of which primitive Simonianism arose, we should interpret the title ἑστώς not in relation to the philosophy of Numenius, where

it refers to the supreme deity,[54] but to such an expression
as in Deuteronomy 5.31: "You stand with me, and I will
tell you all the commandments. . . ." As a prophet like
Moses, Dositheus or Simon has the true commandments of
God.[55]

It may seem surprising that among the adherents of
Dositheus and of Simon the woman Helen was so prominent, but on the one hand women are mentioned in the
Zadokite Document and, on the other, we know that some
of them were buried at Qumran and therefore presumably were members of the community. It should be added
that in the Clementine account there is no trace of the notion that Helen had been a prostitute; this may have been
invented by Christian or Jewish opponents of Simon.

If this analysis is correct, Simonian gnosis arose out of
Judaeo-Samaritan sectarianism, and we can perhaps differentiate various stages in its development. First would come
the period when it was still close to Dositheus and the notion of the "standing one," the prophet like Moses. Then
would come the period when apocalyptic turned into
gnosis, when Simon would come to regard himself, or to be
regarded by his disciples, as the power not of but above
the Creator, and when his fellow-schismatic Helen would
be regarded as "Wisdom, the mother of all." At this point
would come the coordination of Simonianism with the
story of Helen of Troy, and of Simonological doctrine
with Christology.

Only the later stage of Simonian doctrine was known to

the Church Fathers, and this is why they treat Simonianism as the beginning of Gnosticism, ascribing its origins to interest in magic or simply to the paranoiac madness if Simon.

According to two second-century writers, Simon had a disciple who considerably modified his master's teaching; this was Menander, who came from Samaria to teach at Antioch, probably in the reign of Trajan (98–117).[56] It is not really clear why the writers thought of him as Simon's disciple, since all they had in common was enthusiasm for magic and belief in Sophia. Of course, it should be added that, in polemical writing, your magic is my miracle, and vice versa, and furthermore, that the fathers were fond of tracing genetic developments in heresies. Not all their tracings were correct. In any event, the differences between Simon and Menander are striking. Simon was the supreme God; Menander said the supreme God was unknown. Simon said that Helen was Sophia incarnate; Menander did not mention Helen. Simon was Father, Son, and Holy Spirit; Menander said he himself was the Savior. Simon's converts were given grace and hope; Menander provided a baptism which prevented old age and death.

Perhaps Menander supplied a radical demythologizing of Simonianism; in his system every trace of Simon and Helen has disappeared. Instead, there is said to be a magical baptism which rather resembles the Eucharist as described by

Ignatius of Antioch. Ignatius called it a "drug of immortality, an antidote for death" (*Eph.* 20.2). So Menander claimed for his baptism.

But Menander's system may have been misunderstood by his opponents. As Archbishop Carrington suggests, "he may have taught a mystical and spiritual doctrine along the lines of the Pauline sacramentalism," and like Ignatius may have used "the language of poetry, not of theology." [57] Or—and this is also possible—he may have been "de-eschatologizing" Simonianism or the practice of some baptizing sect, perhaps Jewish. If he was really a Simonian, he may have believed that the deaths of Simon and Helen made some adjustments necessary. In any event, the passage of time's winged chariot seems to have ruined his sect, once poetry was taken as prose. Origen tells us, with a reference to the thirty disciples of John the Baptist, that he doubts the existence of thirty Simonians in the whole world,[58] and he does not even mention disciples of Menander.

NON-SIMONIAN ANARCHY

Because of the Simonian emphasis on the merely conventional nature of the Jewish law, we may also discuss some other systems which contained similar views. Before doing so, we should point out, however, that such notions could arise on the borders of either Judaism or Christianity. Philo, for example, held that the Decalogue was the divine expression of the universal law of nature, while some other parts of the Jewish law were nonliteral extensions of it.[59] Similarly some early Christian writers treat the Decalogue as that part of the law which Jesus "fulfilled"; he abrogated the rest of the law.[60] But Gnostics, who rejected the Creator and his creation, could not regard the law of nature any more highly than the rest of the Creator's work.

The Cainites treated Sophia as the mother of those who in the Old Testament are described or can be understood as victims of Yahweh.[61] They therefore regarded violation of his laws as a positive duty. In order to achieve what they called "perfect knowledge," they had to pass through every kind of experience, in transit invoking appropriate angels. Similarly, the Antitactae mentioned by Clement of Alexandria held that while they were "by nature" children of the Father of the All, who made everything good, his adversary was responsible for the Jewish law. "We resist him in order to vindicate the Father, acting against the will of the second one. Since he said, 'Thou shalt not commit adultery,' we should commit it in order to destroy his commandment." [62] And from a relatively early period comes the system ascribed to Carpocrates, in which it was taught that the Jewish law was given by the angels who made the world. Jesus despised it but received divine power by means of which he overcame the passions. Carpocratians, on the other hand, overcome them by experiencing everything. If they cannot achieve total experience in one lifetime, their souls will transmigrate into other bodies until they can achieve it. In their view there is thus a contrast between what Jesus did and what he taught, for their doctrine is based on the teaching of Jesus. "Agree with your adversary quickly," he said (Matt. 5.25), "while you are on the way with him, lest the adversary deliver you to the judge"—the chief of the angels, presumably Yahweh—"and you be cast into prison"—another body. The Carpocratians made use of the Gospel saying, "Give to him who asks" (Matt. 5.42), and we may suppose that "Do not resist evil" (Matt. 5.39) would have been a favorite text.[63] In other words, counsels of eschatological perfection have been transmuted into a kind of Cynicizing gnosis. But these Gnostics went beyond Cynicism when they insisted that to experience everything was a positive duty. This notion comes from hostility to the world, the flesh, and its Creator.

To such Gnostics the Church replied by insisting on the unity of the Old and New Testaments, the Bible which told how the one God made the world, gave his moral law to Moses, and through his prophets predicted the coming of Jesus. For the Church, freedom was freedom from sin and from the details of the Jewish law, not from the Decalogue. In the second century the Church may not have encouraged the work of creative imagination; it was trying to maintain "the faith once delivered to the saints" (Jude 3). We shall later consider (Chapter 6) the gains and losses which resulted from this effort.

4

THE UNKNOWN FATHER

THE EARLIEST Gnostic systems were to some extent systems of reassurance. Patterned after Christianity, Simonianism recognized the presence of God in Simon and in the Simonian. Salvation was achieved by disregarding conventional morality and by setting one's hope on him and on the mother-figure Helen. Compared with the major systems we encounter later, Simonianism was an optimistic, this-worldly religion.

But as we go on to trace the rise of another kind of system, we encounter Gnostics in whose thought there is no reassurance. There is no mother-figure, and the Father is infinitely remote and quite unknown except by Gnostic revelation. He made inferior powers who are responsible for the world as it is. And he is not the god of the Jews; indeed, the god of the Jews is one of the inferior powers. All that has any value in mankind is a divine spark which has descended from the unknown Father; all else will perish.

We have already argued that a good deal of Gnosticism emerged out of the failure of apocalyptic thought. And at this point we can provide an example of this development, in the shadowy portrait of the Jewish Christian Gnostic Cerinthus which the Church Fathers give us. In the first place, Cerinthus is said to have been a Jew. But his Judaism was hardly orthodox, since he held that the supreme Father was unknown, while the god of the Old Testament, the creator and legislator, was an angel. This doctrine reflects extreme pessimism about the condition of the world. It could not have been created by the supreme God. In the second place, Cerinthus, as a Jewish Christian of sorts, held that Jesus was a man, the son of Joseph and Mary. At the time of his baptism the Christ-power descended upon him, and he became Jesus Christ. In the third place, Cerinthus maintained a strong Jewish eschatological doctrine. According to one report, Christ died at the crucifixion, but he has not yet risen; he will rise at the general resurrection. Then he will establish his reign on earth, in the city of Jerusalem, where the elect will enjoy pleasures, banquets, and marriages, and will offer sacrifices. The kingdom will last a thousand years. Afterwards everything will be restored—we do not know in what way.[1]

This singular form of Christian gnosis reflects a radical alteration of the apocalyptic hope. It is no longer based on the Old Testament but on Christian apocalyptic, primarily the Apocalypse of John, which at least one ancient critic ascribed to Cerinthus himself.[2] For the future work of God has been substituted the future work of Christ; for the future kingdom of God has been substituted the future kingdom of Christ. And the god of the Old Testament has been, so to speak, depotentiated. He is no more than an angel. In other words, in this system we see the beginning of a transition from apocalyptic to gnosis. Here both apocalyptic and Gnostic elements are maintained in a kind of uneasy balance which could not last. One or the other had to become predominant.

The necessary step is taken in the system of Saturninus, who taught at Antioch probably in the reign of Hadrian (117–138). In it, as we shall see, there are many Jewish elements. The description of creation is ultimately based on Genesis. The god of the Jews still has an adversary named Satan. But there is no this-worldly eschatology. Apocalyptic has been replaced by gnosis.

Before considering Saturninus directly, we should say something about what we know of the religious situation at Antioch in the period just before him. We know of two teachers there. One was Menander, whose theology we have already discussed (see Chapter 3). It could not possibly have influenced Saturninus, unless perhaps it drove him by reaction into dualism. The other was the Christian bishop Ignatius, who prided himself on his knowledge of affairs celestial and warned his flock not only against Satan but also against some form of heterodox Judaism. Ignatius' warnings prove the existence of the heterodox Judaism out of which Saturninus' doctrine emerged. They also prove that it was so close to some kind of Christianity that the warnings were necessary.

The historical environment of Saturninus was not purely theological, however. It included at least one Jewish revolt against the Romans, in the years 115–117, and perhaps an-

other, in 132–135. Both revolts were disastrous for those
who took part in them. Both revolts, as we have already
pointed out (see Chapter 1), led radical dualist Jews and
Christians to move from apocalyptic toward gnosis, and to
reinterpret the Old Testament in a new way. Examining
the *Heilsgeschichte* of Saturninus we shall find that such a
reinterpretation is what he is trying to provide.[3]

SATURNINUS' SYSTEM

Saturninus radically rewrites the creation story of Genesis,
interpreting it in haggadic fashion. At the beginning of
things a luminous image descended from the "supreme
authority" or the unknown Father. Presumably Saturninus
knows it was luminous because God said, "Let there be
light" (Gen. 1.3). The angels tried to grasp it but could
not do so—just as "the darkness could not grasp the light"
in John 1.5—and it returned above. Then they decided to
copy it, and they said to themselves, "Let us make a man
after the image and after the likeness." Here Saturninus is
relying on Genesis 1.26, where God says, "Let us make
man after *our* image and after *our* likeness." But he has al-
tered the text by deleting the word "our." He must believe
that the word has been interpolated into Genesis, probably
by one or more of the seven angels. He continues his work
of exegesis by noting the difference between the two creation stories in Genesis. Since it is only in the second story
that man, formed out of the dust of the earth, becomes a
living soul (Gen. 2.7), he can say that the angels made

man out of the dust of the earth but were too feeble to finish their work. Their product possessed form, matter, and motion. But it could not stand erect; it lay on the ground, wriggling like a worm.

The notion of Adam's wriggling captivated Gnostic imaginations. It recurs among the Ophites [4] and in a third-century Marcionite system.[5] Much later, it appears in two passages in the Mandaean *Ginza*, where we read that the first man "lay wriggling like a worm in the black waters," [6] and that before the soul entered the human body, the body "lay wriggling without strength." [7] It is hard to tell just where the notion came from. Perhaps Saturninus ascribed Psalm 22.7 to Adam rather than to Christ: "I am a worm and no man." Perhaps he had even observed human babies, who after all are unable to walk or stand upright; they do wriggle.

Fortunately for man, the "power above" took pity on him and sent the "spark of life" into him. This spark "raised him up and made him live"; here Saturninus alludes to the words of Hosea 6.2, which Christians referred to the resurrection of Jesus.[8] The spark must have been the "breath of life" which, according to Genesis 2.7, Yahweh Elohim breathed into man's nostrils so that he "became a living soul." Saturninus is using semiphilosophical terminology when he speaks of "power above" and "spark of life"; but his primary concern is with providing a revised, if hardly standard, version of Genesis.[9]

Thus far in the story we have encountered nothing really dualistic. The angels are weak, but they are not described as wicked. There is a difference between spirit and matter, for after death the spark of life returns above while the other elements which constitute man are dissolved into their material sources. But this is no more than a combination of "dust thou art, and to dust thou shalt return" (Gen. 3.19) and "the dust returns to the earth as it was, and the spirit returns to God who gave it" (Eccl. 12.7). Now suddenly we are informed that the angels "fashioned" two kinds of men, the wicked and the good. What justification can we find in Genesis for this statement? Probably it lies in the mysterious verse (1.27) which says that "in the image of God (Elohim) created he him; male and female created he them." Since Saturninus referred the preceding verse to the work of the angels, evidently treating Elohim as plural, he doubtless understood this verse too as related to what they did. Therefore, the angels made both male and female. And this analysis would be confirmed by the second creation story, where we read that Yahweh Elohim "fashioned" man from the earth and "built" Eve out of Adam.

In other words, it appears that Saturninus regards men as good and women as bad. Such a notion, in nontheological form, could be found in Ecclesiastes. "One man (*adam*) among a thousand have I found, but a woman among all those have I not found" (7.28). "This only have I found, that Elohim made man upright" (7.29). More obviously, it could be found in Genesis itself. Who gave the forbidden fruit to the virtuous Adam? Professor Goodenough has shown me a Jewish magical amulet on which Eve is por-

trayed as handing it to her husband while the serpent looks
on. And it may be added that the notion could occur in
semiphilosophical thought. The *Timaeus* (42b) of Plato
tells us that the first penalty laid on a wicked soul is that
of imprisonment in a female nature. Sages of all kinds agree
that women are at least distracting. The Severian Gnostics
held that Eve was created by Satan,[10] though rabbinic teachers, and the Christian bishop Theophilus of Antioch, rejected such a view.[11]

  Saturninus also taught that only the good have the spark
of life in them. This doctrine too seems to be based on
Genesis (2.7), where we read that Yahweh Elohim breathed
the breath of life into Adam but not into Eve. The wicked,
says Saturninus, are aided not by God but by demons.
Again, Genesis 3.1–5 tells us that Eve was given counsel by
the serpent. And our interpretation of men as the good and
women as the bad is confirmed by the further statement
that marriage and reproduction come from Satan.

  How does Saturninus know this? Once more, we are involved in rabbinic exegesis of Genesis. In Genesis 4.1 we
read that "Adam knew Eve his wife; and she conceived,
and bore Cain, and said, 'I have gotten a man with
Yahweh.' " In Hebrew, Eve's statement presents some difficulties, and the Old Testament scholar Karl Budde went
so far as to translate it as "I have gotten Yahweh for a
husband." He pointed out that in the *Targum of Pseudo-
Jonathan* her words are rendered, "I have the angel of
Yahweh as my husband."[12] And Wilhelm Bacher added
that in the rather late *Sayings of Rabbi Eliezer* the evil

angel Sammael, often identified with Satan, is regarded as the father of Cain.[13] Here, then, is where Saturninus probably started—with haggadic exegesis of the story of the birth of Cain. In his system Cain was probably the son of Satan.

It should be added that many Christians and Gnostics were fascinated by the serpent's relation to Eve in Eden. The apostle Paul speaks of her seduction by the serpent (2 Cor. 11.2–3), perhaps in a metaphorical way. The Protevangelium of James refers to it as literal (13.1). The apologist Justin allegorizes. "The uncorrupted virgin Eve conceived the word which was from the serpent, and bore disobedience and death." [14] But Gnostics took the notion more literally. It occurs among the Ophites, the Sethians, the Cainites, and the Archontics, as well as in the Gnostic book Baruch.[15] The Apocryphon of John tells us that the evil creator Ialdabaoth-Saclas had intercourse with Eve and begot both the unrighteous Yahweh and the righteous Elohim.[16] Saturninus probably held a similar view.

So much for the story of creation. What of the history of the world in the interim between creation and redemption? In this period, according to Saturninus, the demons, or wicked angels, continued to help the wicked in their conflict with the good. Satan presumably continued to advocate marriage and reproduction. Women presumably continued to oppress men. The world-creating angels, along with Satan himself, inspired Moses and the other Hebrew prophets and thus led mankind astray. The human situation was therefore one of ignorance and slavery. Bad as it was, it was on the verge of becoming worse; for all the "archons" finally joined together and planned to destroy the Father. They were undertaking an assault on the "supreme authority" above. Now how does Saturninus know that they had this plan?

Once more, we turn to the Old Testament. According to Isaiah (14.12–15), the morning star—obviously, for a Gnostic, a planetary spirit—said in his heart, "I will ascend into heaven, I will exalt my throne above the stars of Elohim." In Ezekiel (28.2–19), a Gnostic could read that an "archon" who had formerly been in the paradise of Elohim said, "I am Elohim; I dwell in the dwelling of Elohim." And such exegesis would be validated by a consideration of the second Psalm, read with eyes of Gnostic faith. In the Septuagint version we read that "the kings of the earth rose up and the archons took counsel together against the Lord and against his Christ." Less imaginative Christians had already found a "king" in Herod Antipas and an "archon" in Pontius Pilate (Acts 4.27). But since the apostle Paul had apparently regarded the "archons" as demonic powers which crucified Christ (1 Cor. 2.8), the way was open for Saturninus to interpret them as planetary angels. From Jewish and Christian apocalyptic he was aware of a warfare in heaven.[17]

Because of this crisis in heaven, a notion derived by Saturninus from previous apocalyptic doctrine, the Savior, also known as Christ, descended from heaven. Presumably it was as Christ that he descended to destroy the god of the Jews, and as Savior to destroy wicked men and their demonic allies. He came to save those who believe in him, the good who have the spark of life in themselves. Now what could this descent mean in relation to the life of mankind? It must mean that, as we read in the Gospel of the Egyptians, the Savior came to "destroy the works of the female," to bring marriage and reproduction to an end, to save men from women.[18]

Christians may suppose that the Savior was human as well as divine, or that "the Logos became flesh" (John 1.14). Their faith is false. The Savior was actually unbegotten, incorporeal, and formless. Those who thought he was a man were wrong, since he simply had the appearance of being a man. Here Saturninus could appeal to a famous passage in Isaiah (53.2) which says that the servant of God "has no form." The servant had already been identified with Christ by Christians. And he could also appeal to a passage in the Pauline Epistles which from a Gnostic's point of view is at least unguarded. This is the "hymn of Christ," found in Philippians (2.6–11). In it Saturninus could read that Christ "assumed the form of a slave" and "came to be in the likeness of men" and "appeared in human form." From these expressions he could easily conclude that the Savior was not actually a man. His view would be reinforced by the great gulf existing between the supreme authority in heaven and man as the creation of the angels. The Savior came to save those who believed him. Here Saturninus is close to the early Christian conception of salvation as the consequence of faith, as we shall see. But only the good, who have the divine spark, do believe.

What does the follower of Saturninus do at the present time, while he presumably is waiting for his own divine spark to return above? He probably knows that the Savior has already returned above, as in the Gospel of John, and, probably, on the ground of what the Savior said is some secret revelation, he knows how to understand the history of the universe. Meanwhile he knows; he is a Gnostic. He knows that he has, and essentially *is*, the divine spark. He can hold that whatever he does in the body is a matter of indifference, but in Saturninus' system he must avoid whatever would defile the spark and place him under the power of the demons. Since the Savior has taught that marriage and reproduction come from Satan, he will avoid both. He will practice the "continence" recommended by Plato, Philo, the Essenes, and Paul, though not all followers of Saturninus hold that such continence requires abstinence from meat. The nonabstainers could agree with Paul that eating meat and not eating it are matters of indifference (1 Cor. 8.8). Perhaps we may suspect that a measure of laxity has slipped into the doctrine of some followers of Saturninus.

When we examine his system as a whole, it is fairly clear that it is a combination of Platonism and anti-Semitism with apocalyptic, haggadic Judaism and Christianity. Yet it is not the combination or the urge to create a combination which creates the system. It is the feeling of hostility toward the world, toward the world-accepting Jews, toward the world-creating, sex-creating god of the Jews, which drives Saturninus into his speculations. And such a system is no product of the study, of quiet speculation on the meaning of the universe. It is a system which is rooted and grounded in revelation. This revelation supplants other revelations. It makes plain the fact that the Old Testament prophecies are the work of angels, some bad, some worse.

We must therefore insist that Saturninus did not consciously create this system but must have believed that he had received it from the Savior. Who was the Savior from whom he received it? According to Irenaeus, our only ancient source of information on this subject, Saturninus was the successor of Simon and Menander. But while there are resemblances to Simonianism in Saturninus' cosmology, and while his teaching about the first power unknown to all is like that of Menander, there is a basic difference between his system and theirs. In Simonianism salvation is liberation from convention, from the moral laws arbitrarily decreed by the angels. Salvation comes from faith in Simon and Helen and from Simon's grace; but it is a this-worldly salvation. Menander came for the salvation of men, and gave them a baptism which makes his disciples deathless, ageless, and immortal. They live on in this world and overcome the angels here. Indeed, the use of the word "magician" to describe both Simon and Menander is an indication of the same thing. Magic is a this-worldly art, a kind of science which gives power here and now. Of magic in relation to Saturninus there is no trace whatever. Finally, Simon regarded himself as the supreme god, and Menander said that he himself was the Savior sent from above. Thus both Simon and Menander had no need of revelation; they *were* revelation. Saturninus was not a revealer but a Gnostic teacher. He therefore needed some revelation which might be given him.

THE APOCRYPHON OF JOHN

Now it is only very recently that we have come to possess the text of a revelation which is at least close to what Saturninus taught, and since in its present Coptic form it is no earlier than the fifth century, we cannot be sure that in every respect it represents Saturninus' system. I should certainly not say, as I once did, that Saturninus wrote this revelation, even though in some respects it resembles his system. I refer to the Apocryphon (or secret teaching) of John, discovered more than sixty years ago, but first published by Walter Till in 1955. The origins of the work can be traced much earlier than the fifth century, however, since something very much like it was used by Irenaeus when he described the system of the Sethian-Ophites. The work therefore comes from a time well within the second century, though details were doubtless modified as it was transmitted.

The Apocryphon begins with the statement that it contains a revelation given by one who is the Father, the Mother, and the Son; but at the end of the book it is plain that the real revealer is either Christ or the Savior. After a description of various emanations from the first imperishable Aeon, we finally come to the creation of the world by Ialdabaoth, presumably the inferior god whom Saturninus calls the "god of the Jews." Seven archons of Ialdabaoth see a reflection of the Aeon in the water—presumably the

water of Genesis 1.2—and they say to one another, "Let
us make a man, after the image and after the likeness of
God." They make man's body, and even his soul, but he
remains inert (like Adam in rabbinic speculation); [19] the
archons and their assistants cannot raise him up. Then
Ialdabaoth, who has received some Spirit from his Mother
above, breathes it into him, and man moves; finally, "the
blessed Father" sends his own Spirit to help this divine
spirit in man. Ialdabaoth remains hostile. He places man in
paradise to lead him astray; later he seduces Eve and
generates Cain and Abel, whose real names are Yahweh and
Elohim. Some men have the Spirit of Life; others have received the Imitation Spirit because of the union of Ialdabaoth's angels with the daughters of men (Gen. 6.1). Those
who have the Spirit of Life will rise upward to the great
lights above, and will inherit eternal life.

This is not exactly the system of Saturninus. It tells much
more about the emanations of the aeons than he does. And
there are details which are different from those Saturninus
gives. In Saturninus' view, a power from above sends a
spark into wriggling Adam; in the Apocryphon, it is
Ialdabaoth who breathes spirit into inert Adam. But this
difference does not amount to much. In the Apocryphon
Irenaeus knew, Adam wriggled.[20] And the theological
methods of the Apocryphon and of Saturninus are much
the same. Both the Apocryphon and Saturninus set forth
the words of revelation. And neither hesitates to correct the
incorrect account given by Moses. Saturninus ascribes
prophecy to the angels; in the Apocryphon we often read

that the true account is "not as Moses said." The Apocryphon and Saturninus share a common hostility toward the world, the flesh, and the god of the Jews, though Saturninus still retains a Jewish Christian idea when he treats Satan as the adversary of the god of the Jews; in the Apocryphon Ialdabaoth and Saclas, the devil, are the same.

How are these resemblances and differences to be explained? It seems likely that the revelation in its earliest form is that set forth by Saturninus. In it there is no mention of the female principle Sophia, though, of course, we have met her under the name of Ennoia, "thought," in Simon and Menander. There is, in other words, no great Mother in the ascetic dualism of Saturninus. On the other hand, the Mother plays a fairly prominent role in the Apocryphon, and (as far as one can see) disturbs the symmetry of something like the system of Saturninus. We should therefore be inclined to see in the Apocryphon a later fusion of a Father-system with a Mother-system.

We thus agree with Quispel in regarding the Apocryphon as containing a relatively late form of the Gnostic myth, though our analysis is somewhat different from his, since he starts with Sophia, and finds that the interpolated element is Ialdabaoth.[21] The difference, however, is more apparent than real, since we should agree that both a Father-system and a Mother-system are prior to the Apocryphon of John as it actually is.

Saturninus, then, is an important witness to the formation of Gnostic systems out of previously existing philosophical and religious phenomena. He is an equally important witness to the presence of Christian influence on this process. Saturninus, unlike Simon and Menander, could not have taught his pupils had he not explicitly made use of a tradition earlier than himself. He must have held that somehow his revelation had come to him from the Savior-Christ. Perhaps, like the author of the Apocryphon of John, he taught that he had received it from a postresurrection appearance of Jesus. In any event, Saturninus was more obviously a Christian Gnostic than either Simon or Menander had been.

But Christianity is only one element in the doctrine of Saturninus. In order to assess its importance we must look more closely at the sources of his system and inquire how he made use of them.

SATURNINUS' SOURCES

The Dead Sea Scrolls have reminded scholars of what they already knew, or should have known. There was a strong ethical dualism in late Judaism, where we encounter the two spirits of light and darkness which presumably go back to the ancient religion of Iran. In Judaism it was essential to modify the Iranian idea by holding that both spirits were created by the one God, and this is the modification we meet in the scrolls. Though the dualism is often more stringent in Gnosticism, many Gnostics still hold that both good and evil are ultimately derived from the unknown Father.

The development of this dualism has been set forth schematically by Professor K. G. Kuhn of Göttingen.[22]

The ethical and eschatological dualism of the preaching of
Zarathustra and of the later Iranian religion found acceptance in
this Palestinian, late Jewish community [Qumran], and was
combined with its Old Testament foundation, while gnosis
represents a *later* stage of the infiltration of Parsee dualism. In
this stage it was revised, under the wholly different influence of
Greek thought, into a physical dualism of substance. In this
way for the first time there arose the notion, decisive for gnosis,
that *matter*, the world in terms of its physical substance, is the
enemy of God.

In other words, in gnosis (by which Kuhn means the kind
of system set forth by Saturninus) there are three elements:
Judaism based on the Old Testament, Iranian dualism, and
a kind of Greek thought which also verges on dualism. It
is the Greek element which differentiates gnosis from
earlier Jewish-Iranian (i.e., apocalyptic) dualism.

As we examine the system of Saturninus we shall see
that Kuhn's analysis is largely correct. But it needs some
modification. We can treat Judaism and Iranian dualism
together and speak simply of haggadic, apocalyptic, dualistic exegesis of the Old Testament. This, we should say,
is the first and perhaps the most important element in
Saturninus' thought. Second, we shall find some Greek
elements in his system, though we should not agree that
the hostility of matter toward God is the most important
of them. And finally, we have already mentioned the importance of Christian thinking about Jesus as a factor of
great significance in the doctrine.

1) The most important of the materials Saturninus uses
are those derived from the Old Testament. Of course, by
"Old Testament" I do not mean what ancient Church

Fathers or modern historical critics would find in it. We must look at the Old Testament as Saturninus looked at it. (*a*) We must not think of the Old Testament as a Christian book. That is to say, we must rid ourselves of any notion that the Old Testament prophecies refer to Jesus or to the Church, for Gnostics know that Christians generally are incapable of understanding revelation. (*b*) We must also refrain from analyzing the Old Testament by means of literary or historical criticism. We Gnostics do not recognize the work of J, E, D, or P; we know by revelation that various angels inspired various prophets. We reject the unity of the Bible, though we use the haggadic exegetical method, searching for obscure passages and finding points of departure for our doctrine of various cosmic powers. We use rabbinic exegesis against the rabbis.

But how can we find dualism in such a book as Genesis? Here we must add to the Old Testament the influence of late Jewish thought. And to describe it I am going to borrow some words of Sigmund Mowinckel.[23]

In its religious structure, the eschatology of later Judaism actually reveals a more extreme form of dualism than that of Persia. . . . Persian eschatology presents us with a conflict between good and evil, in which man can freely take sides, and contribute to the result, God's victory over the evil power which, for some inexplicable reason, has existed from the beginning. In the eschatology of . . . later Judaism, we find an entire re-creation of mankind and nature which, as the result of a fall and of the sin which has become their nature, have come under the power of evil, and would be destroyed if God did not intervene with his miracle of restoration.

Speculative apocalyptic-minded Jewish exegetes had already reinterpreted Genesis along lines like these, and it was easy enough for those who used their method to make use of some of their results and transform them into gnosis.

At the same time, these gnostics made use of certain aspects of Greek thought.

2) By "Greek thought" we mean primarily Platonism, for in the first and second centuries of our era Platonism was becoming more and more religious and was thus available for theologians' use as other systems were not. Among the doctrines which Gnostics would find especially congenial there was the cosmological teaching of Albinus, who, following Plato, tells us that the planets are gods; there are seven of them, and in the eighth place is the "power from above" which encompasses the others. Then there was teaching about the nature of man. Following the *Timaeus*, Albinus says that the Demiurge assigned the creation of men to gods inferior to himself, for if he himself had made men, they would have been immortal. These lower gods made men out of the elements; the Demiurge sent down souls for them. The body, made by the lower gods, is the seat of the affections, such as sense-perception and the emotions of pleasure, grief, fear, and anger; only the soul, the gift of the Demiurge, is immortal.[24]

Finally, in another form of Platonism, expressed by Numenius of Apamea, the highest god is separated from the Demiurge.[25] An analogy to this doctrine is already provided by Philo, who speaks of the Logos as a "second God" and says that "the Logos is the God of us imperfect men, but the primal God is the God of the wise and perfect." [26]

All these elements could have been, and probably were, employed by Gnostics in their descriptions of the origin of the world and of man. We have encountered all of them, or something like them, in the system of Saturninus.

3) So there are elements from the Old Testament and from Greek thought in the system of Saturninus. In this regard it is like the work of Philo, in which the Old Testament, and some haggadic exegesis, is interpreted along lines at least semiphilosophical. But there is another element in Saturninus' thought which is not like Philo. This consists of ideas borrowed, in more or less distorted form, from Christianity. As we have already said, the Savior of Saturninus is Jesus. He merely seemed to be a man, as unorthodox Christians said. He came to destroy demons, as the Synoptic Gospels point out (Mark 1.24; Luke 4.34). He came to "destroy the works of the devil" (1 John 3.8); and since Saturninus could easily have read the Gospel of John, he could learn from it that the devil was the Father of the Jews (8.44); so, he could conclude, Jesus came to destroy the god of the Jews.

At another point Saturninus seems to be indebted to Christian doctrine. In his myth he told us that the angels made two classes of men, the wicked and the good. Yet in his picture of salvation he says that the Savior came to save those who believe him and have the spark of life in them.[27] This idea too seems to reflect the Pauline and Johannine combination of determinism and free-will. In John, faith and knowledge are coordinated (for example, John 17.8), and believers are described as "not of this world" (17.16). Jesus came to give life to those who were capable of receiving it (see 17.2).

Behind, or at any rate in, the thought of Saturninus and of the Apocryphon there seems to be a common core of dualistic reinterpretation of the Old Testament and of the story of Jesus. And out of this common core came the various dualistic systems such as those of the Ophites, the Sethians, the Naassenes, and the Archontics. Perhaps we should not speak of Saturninus as distinct from the Ophites. Irenaeus makes such a distinction, but as George Salmon long ago pointed out, he may do so simply because he uses different sources to describe the same system.[28] There are many minor differences among the various dualistic systems, but they have this in common: all of them are sharply opposed to the god of the Jews, sometimes called "the accursed god of the Jews," and most of them venerate his adversary, the serpent in the garden of Eden (hence the names "Ophites" from ὄφις and "Naassenes" from נחש).

The Ophites whom the anti-Christian writer Celsus knew explained why this god was accursed: he sends rain and thunder; he created the world; he is the god of Moses. These explanations seem rather unequal in value. The ancients were often afraid of thunder, but most of them were aware that rain is beneficial. Perhaps the Ophites were thinking of the rain which Yahweh used to make the flood. A more adequate theological explanation was this: he deserves to be cursed because he himself cursed the serpent, which gave the first man the knowledge of good and evil. The extent of the Ophites' dualism is startlingly attested by Origen himself, who says that they curse Jesus and do not admit converts until they have cursed him too.[29] Presumably by "Jesus" the Ophites were referring to the flesh-and-blood Jesus of Nazareth, whom they rejected in favor of their Savior-Christ.

It is evident that by the time we have reached this point in the dualistic development we are a long way from any form of Judaism. Indeed, it is fairly plain that all these Gnostics are radically anti-Semitic. Yet they continue to rewrite the Old Testament. They seem almost obsessed by the theological problem which it poses. This feature of their thought has been explained as proof of their Jewish origin. The most militant anti-Semites, it is said, are ex-Jews. There may or may not be something to this theory. But in antiquity, at any rate, the most militant anti-Semites were gentiles.[30] And what seems to have happened is that a movement which may well have begun in Judaism, or rather in a reaction against and out of (specifically) apocalyptic Judaism, soon attracted adherents who were not Jews but gentiles. Like Christianity, this kind of gnosis began in heterodox Judaism but ended in the world of Greco-Roman syncretism.[31]

Christianity was saved from dualistic gnosis, in so far as it was saved, because it insisted upon retaining the Old Testament more or less as it stood, and thereby retained the doctrine of the goodness of the created world. While

Christianity encouraged asceticism, partly because of its own apocalyptic origins, it did not insist upon it for all. And its doctrine of the unity and omnipotence of God meant that the created world was under his control.

5

FROM MYTH TO PHILOSOPHY?

IN THE early Gnostic systems we have been dis-
cussing, one of the most conspicuous features is mythology.
The Simonians tell a myth of pre-existent Wisdom; Saturninus tells a myth which is reinterpretation of the creation myth of the book of Genesis. Now it has been argued
by some highly competent scholars, such as Rudolf Bultmann and Hans Jonas, that in the great Gnostic schools of
the mid-second century a process of "demythologizing"
takes place. Myth comes to be "spiritualized"; it is interpreted in philosophical, or at least semiphilosophical,
terms. This claim is one of the foundation stones for these
scholars' method of reading back later mythology, such
as that preserved among the Mandaeans, into earlier times.
For this reason we must carefully examine the development
of the thought of some of the great Gnostic teachers. We
must try to see whether it really begins in mythology and
ends in philosophy,[1] or (to use Wilhelm Nestle's phrase)
proceeds *Vom Mythos zum Logos.*

We should enter a caveat before we begin, by pointing
out that in any event there was no straight-line development. There was a great deal of wild mythology in the

third century: *Pistis Sophia* and the *Books of Ieû* and in
many of the systems alive, or half-alive, in 374 when
Epiphanius began to compile his collection of heresies.
Manichaeism is exceedingly mythological; so is Mandaean
gnosis. If demythologizing took place, it certainly did not
touch many Gnostic groups.

Now we shall proceed to discuss the thought of Marcion,
who came from Pontus to Rome about 139; his con-
temporary Valentinus, who also taught at Rome; some of
Valentinus' followers; Basilides, who earlier taught at
Alexandria; and finally the philosopher Numenius of
Apamea, sometimes associated with Gnosticism by modern
writers; and the collection of writings known as the
Hermetica.

MARCION AND THE CHURCH OF ROME

We begin with Marcion for several reasons. Most important
is the fact that some modern scholars have thought of him
as a prototype of biblical critics in the nineteenth and
twentieth centuries. Didn't he reject the Old Testament and
try to delete interpolations from the teaching of Jesus and
Paul? It is certainly true that he did. But I think it would
be better to look at Marcion in his second-century context
before making symbolical use of him for more modern
times.

At least part of Marcion's ministry can be dated with
fair accuracy. He came from Pontus, on the south shore
of the Black Sea, to Rome during the episcopate of

Hyginus, roughly between 136 and 140. He was expelled from the Roman church in the year 144. Now the time of his arrival suggests pretty strongly what the occasion of his coming was. The last and most disastrous of the Jewish apocalyptic revolts had ended in 135 with a thoroughgoing massacre of Jews in the eastern part of the empire. And Marcion took current events very seriously; he tried to see what their theological significance was. Under these circumstances he wanted to dissociate Christianity not only from apocalyptic Judaism but also from Judaism in general. He wanted to show that the Jewish elements in the Christian tradition were only secondary and that they should be removed.

It is significant that he wanted to provide this demonstration for the Christian church at Rome. What do we know about Roman Christianity in Marcion's time? Admittedly the evidence is rather poor in quantity. But most of it points toward the presence of a strongly Jewish Christianity in the Roman church. The letter of the Roman church to the Corinthians, written nearly half a century earlier, is based largely on the Old Testament and partly on the teaching of Jesus and Paul. Its author interprets this combination in an environment which seems predominantly that of Hellenistic Judaism. Somewhat later, we find the collection of visions, commandments, and allegorical parables composed by a Roman Christian named Hermas. The basic concern of Hermas is with ethics, Jewish ethics, and the semiphilosophical interests of the Roman letter to the Corinthians have disappeared. Indeed, the moral teaching

of Hermas is so Jewish, and so similar to that of some of the
Dead Sea Scrolls, that a modern scholar has argued that
Hermas cannot possibly represent the mainstream of
Roman Christianity in his time.[2] Moreover, his theology,
such as it is, is thoroughly Jewish. The Son of God is
identified with the Holy Spirit, with the Name of God,
and with the Law of God. The Law of God is put into
men's hearts by the "great and glorious angel" Michael,
who at some points seems to be identified with the Son.
Hermas never mentions either Jesus or Christ. What he tells
us of the incarnation is that God made the Holy Spirit
dwell in a flesh which he had chosen; this flesh served the
Spirit well and therefore, after the Spirit had left it, God
gave the flesh a "place of tabernacling" as a reward
(Sim. 5.6). Presumably the coming of the Spirit made Jesus
become Jesus Christ, though Hermas does not say so.

Another document which probably represents Roman
Christianity in the early second century is the homily
known as 2 Clement, in which we find many ideas which
are close to those of Hermas. But the author of 2 Clement
seems to have been more subject to Gnostic, or semi-
Gnostic, thought than Hermas had been. He makes use
of a saying of Jesus apparently derived from the Gospel of
the Egyptians, even though he provides exegesis of it in
order to make it more orthodox than it originally was
(12.2–6). He speculates on the meaning of Genesis 1.27
("God made man male and female") and says that "the
male is Christ, the female is the Church"—both are pre-
existent spiritual beings (14.1–2). Finally, unlike any other

early orthodox writer, the author of 2 Clement speaks of
God as "the Father of Truth" (3.1; 20.5)—an appellation
frequently used by the Valentinians.[3] 2 Clement is not
Gnostic, but it comes out of an environment where
Gnosticism is not wholly rejected.

A similar situation is reflected in what Irenaeus tells us
about Roman heterodoxy before Marcion (and Valentinus)
flourished. At Rome there was a Gnostic teacher named
Cerdo, who secretly taught that the God of the Old Testament was just and was known from his revelation; the
Father of Jesus, on the other hand, was good, and Jesus
had first made him known. Cerdo's work had been rather
unsuccessful. Every so often his teaching would be discovered and he would be expelled. Then he would publicly
recant and be received back again. Then the whole process
would start anew.[4] Irenaeus says that when Marcion came
to Rome he fell under Cerdo's influence and was led
astray. It is possible, however, that Marcion had already
developed similar ideas.[5] At the very least, he was ready
to be led astray.

But what kind of ideas had Cerdo been expressing? It
looks as if the conflict within the Roman church had involved two different forms of Jewish Christian theology.
That represented by Hermas was a synthetic, almost
mystical, kind of theology in which correlations among
angels and names were very important. That represented
by Cerdo was a more rationalistic theology which tried to
make distinctions between names. Philo is our earliest
witness to this kind of analysis. He tells us that in the Old

Testament the name "Lord" (a translation of Yahweh) refers to God's activity as creator and judge, while "God" (a translation of Elohim) refers to his goodness and mercy.[6] What Cerdo and Marcion did was to transfer this distinction from the Old Testament to the story of Jesus. They could have said that the God of the Old Testament was Yahweh, while the Father of Jesus was Elohim. But in transferring the distinction they also transformed it. They ended up with two gods rather than one. Cerdo, or for that matter Marcion, may well have been acquainted with Syrian gnosis, as we shall see. In any event, the notion of two gods rather than one is Gnostic. It ultimately involves the rejection of the Old Testament as the revelation of an inferior god.

Now Harnack, who was a great enthusiast for Marcion, claimed that he was not a Gnostic at all.[7] He pointed out the basically Christian character of many of Marcion's beliefs. For example, Marcion insisted on the need of faith (not gnosis) in the God who revealed himself only in Christ. He made no use of non-biblical myths or of a secret tradition (with one exception, which we shall discuss later). He taught nothing about the fall or ascent of the soul or the spirit; in his view, salvation was available for all men, and it did not involve the use of magical rites.

All this we can readily admit. But Harnack also drew attention to some very Gnostic features of Marcion's teaching. These include rejecting the Old Testament, separating the supreme unknown God from the Creator and Legislator, treating matter as evil, rejecting the hu-

manity of Jesus and the resurrection of the flesh, and
recommending militant asceticism. These features are all
characteristic of the dualistic gnosis of Syria. They may
have come to Marcion from Cerdo, who according to
Epiphanius [8] came from Syria and was influenced by
Saturninus (see Chapter 4).

And we should also mention a singular bit of mythology
which Irenaeus says Marcion believed. According to this
story, when Jesus descended into Hades the sinners there
gladly heard him and were saved, but the saints thought
that as usual their God was testing them; they therefore
rejected salvation.[9] This bit of Marcionite theology
strongly resembles the Old Testament exegesis of the
Cainite Gnostics (see Chapter 2).

The system of Marcion looks like a combination of
Christianity and Syrian gnosis. Which element was first?
The answer seems to be that Marcion was originally a
Christian; at any rate, Tertullian mentions an early letter
of his which seemed quite orthodox.[10] But when he came
to Rome he found that Cerdo's Gnosticism fitted quite well
into a theological scheme he had long had in mind. He proceeded to write his books: his revised editions of the Gospel
and the Apostle, and his Antitheses.

In the historical situation resulting from the second
Jewish revolt and the consequent spread of anti-Semitism,
he believed that he could prove that the inconsistencies of
the Christian tradition were due to interpolations by
Judaizers. From the Synoptic Gospels he could learn that
the earlier disciples misunderstood Jesus, and he could

conclude that only Paul understood him, though Paul's own letters had been interpolated. He could then proceed to argue that the authentic Gospel had been given Paul by revelation. Key texts were provided by Galatians and Romans, and by a passage in 1 Corinthians (11.23) where Paul says he received his account of the Last Supper "from the Lord." [11] Since an identical account appears only in the Gospel of Luke, it was obvious that this Gospel must have been Paul's. Marcion thereupon undertook to remove Judaizing interpolations from this Gospel.

It is barely possible that Marcion could have made this philological reconstruction on the basis of the New Testament materials alone. It is much more probable, however, that the impetus for discovering interpolations was provided by a point of view at first implicitly Gnostic and later, under Cerdo's influence, explicitly so.

We need not deny that Marcion thought he was recovering authentic Christianity. This too was a common Gnostic belief. And in the time when he came to Rome, a good many Christians undoubtedly agreed with him. They were not accustomed to systematic theology or to philological method, and they were grateful for his gift of 200,000 sesterces. By the year 144, however, the administrators of the Roman church were fully aware of the un-biblical, unhistorical nature of his teaching, and they excommunicated him.[12] Theological leadership in this movement was probably provided by the philosophically minded Justin, who had recently come to Rome and produced the treatise *Against All Heresies*. In any event, we know that in his

Apology, written around 150, Justin refers to this prior
work, and we do not know of any other Christian writer
who so early attacked Marcion's doctrine.

Marcion tried to create a meaningful Christianity by
purging it of its Jewish elements, including apocalyptic
eschatology. As he did so, he fell under the influence of
Syrian dualistic gnosis. But his was not the only new
interpretation which Roman Christians encountered in the
middle of the second century.

VALENTINUS AND THE GOSPEL OF TRUTH

In Marcion's time there came to Rome another Gnostic
teacher with a very different kind of gnosis. Where
Marcion had met Jewish Christianity in a head-on collision
and had tried to "de-Judaize" Christian theology, Valentinus built on the religious foundations already laid.
Indeed, such building was characteristic of the Valentinian
school. There are strong resemblances between the speculations of the *Shepherd of Hermas* and Valentinus' Gospel
of Truth; at certain key points the views of the apologist
Justin and the Valentinian Ptolemaeus converge; and in
dealing with the views of the Valentinian Theodotus,
Clement of Alexandria often writes them down without
criticism.

The Gospel of Truth, first published in 1957, is full of
Jewish mystical speculation and lacks any explicit criticism
of the Jews or of Jewish Christianity. It suggests that
Valentinus was trying to reinterpret Jewish apocalyptic

Christianity as Jewish Gnostic Christianity, and that the occasion for his work, as for that of Marcion, was the apocalyptic catastrophe in the reign of Hadrian.

Van Unnik has shown that in the *Gospel* are to be found echoes of nearly all the New Testament writings, except the Pastoral Epistles.[13] This means, I think, that Valentinus was providing a reinterpretation of Christian doctrine. He was setting forth the further revelation which had already been promised in the Gospel of John, his favorite Gospel. For in that Gospel we read that when the Paraclete comes he will lead Christians into the whole truth, a truth which the disciples of Jesus were not yet ready to hear.[14] Later Valentinians, and probably Valentinus himself at a later time, proceeded to create systems, just as later Christians did. But in the Gospel of Truth the stage of systematic theology has not been reached; we are concerned simply with revelation.

The Gospel of Truth announces itself as "joy for those who from the Father of Truth have received him who through the power of the Word came forth from the Pleroma, him who is immanent in the Mind of the Father, him who is called the Savior." Then it goes on to describe the early development of ignorance and error. Originally the Father contained everything, including the aeons he had produced. But somehow (p. 22.27)—Valentinus does not say just how—they did not know him; they were in ignorance, and Error, Anguish, Oblivion, and Terror came into existence. Error "elaborated its own matter in the void, without knowing Truth; it applied itself to the modeling of a creature, trying to provide in beauty the equivalent of Truth" (p. 17.15). The state of this creature, or the "place" in which it is, is Deficiency, caused by ignorance of the Father (p. 24.25). Men in this place were unstable and torn asunder; their life was like a nightmare (p. 29).

Most of the Gospel discusses the meaning of redemption, frequently reinterpreting passages from the New Testament. Jesus the Christ (p. 18.16), "the merciful and faithful one" (p. 20.10), "the beloved Son" (p. 30.31), the embodied Word (p. 26.4), and the Name of God (pp. 38–40), came to reveal to the aeons the gnosis of the living Book (p. 22.38), to teach, to suffer, and to die (p. 20.10, 25). He appeared and taught in the midst of a school (p. 19.18), just as the boy Jesus taught in the temple (Luke 2.46). False sages tested and hated him, but little children came to him (p. 19.25), just as in the Gospel of Matthew (19.3, 13). At his death he "divested himself of these perishable rags, he clothed himself in imperishability" (p. 20.30). The Holy Spirit, "the tongue of the Father" (p. 26.35), revivified him. "Having helped him who was stretched out upon the ground"—like the first Adam in Syrian Gnostic thought—"it placed him on his feet, for truly he had not yet reappeared" (p. 30.19). He became a Way (John 14.6), a Gnosis, a Discovery, and a Confirmation (p. 31.28). He is the Shepherd (p. 31.35; John 10.11), who left 99 sheep to seek one (Luke 15.4).

The result of Jesus' coming is that Gnostics, who meditate on the Name of God (p. 40.5), recognize that their root is in him (p. 41.17); they "strain toward that unique

One" (p. 42.15), and they do not descend into Hades
(p. 42.17). The Father is in them, and they are in the
Father (p. 42.27; John 14.10–11; 17.22).

Valentinus does not describe the fate of material men,
who presumably do descend into Hades. "May they know,"
he concludes, "each in his own place, that it does not suit
me, after having sojourned in the Place of Rest, to say
anything more. But I shall be in it in order to devote myself at all times to the Father of the All and to the true
brothers" (p. 42.39). These true brothers "manifest themselves truly since they are in true and eternal life" (p. 43.9).

This fascinating doctrine is obviously close to Christianity, especially that presented in the Johannic Gospel
and epistles. Yet, while there is no clear separation of the
Father from the Creator, Error is evidently a surrogate for
the latter; it "elaborated its own matter," and it was only
imitating Truth when it modeled a creature. Some dualism
is latent here, even though it is not clearly expressed. Again,
while Jesus was really "annihilated" (p. 18.24) when he
was "nailed to a cross" (pp. 18.24; 20.25), and really suffered (p. 20.11), after his resurrection he "came in flesh
of similitude" (p. 31.4); "nothing could obstruct its
course" (p. 31.5; see also John 20.19, 26). And behind the
Gospel of Truth lies the doctrine of the aeons, of their
fall, of their control of the world. Behind it lies also the
doctrine that the Gnostic is a being from on high, unlike
material men. And the Gnostic lives even now in the
heavenly Place of Rest. Like the Fourth Evangelist, Valentinus has reduced the role of apocalyptic eschatology.

Is this his original doctrine? Tertullian suggests that it is when he tells us that while Valentinus personified abstractions within the nature of God, while his pupil Ptolemaeus developed a more mythological system.[15]

What else can be said of the liturgical or devotional reading of the communities created by Valentinus? We know that he wrote psalms, and a fragment of one of them has been preserved by Hippolytus.[16] It contains a description of a "chain of being" which Valentinus saw in spiritual vision. But it may be possible to find other psalms which he, or other early Valentinians, wrote.

When Rendel Harris published his *editio princeps* of the *Odes of Solomon* in 1909, he was much impressed by the mysteriousness of Ode 23, which describes the reception of a letter from heaven. As he said (p. 121), "some book may have been published, claiming Divine Authority. . . . It appeared suddenly, unexpectedly, and met with opposition rather than universal acceptance. . . . [It] conveyed a message to those below from one above, and it interpreted the region below to include the invisible world. . . . It contained some pronounced statement concerning the Trinity, for we are expressly told that it had the name of Father, Son, and Holy Ghost upon it."

The Ode begins with these words:

Joy is of the saints, and who shall put it on but they alone?
Grace is of the elect, and who shall receive it but those who
    trust in it from the beginning?
Love is of the elect, and who shall put it on but those who have
    possessed it from the beginning?
Walk in the knowledge of the Most High. . . .

Now when we turn to the Gospel of Truth, we find that
it begins as follows:

The Gospel of Truth is *joy* for those who have received the
grace of *knowing* from the Father of Truth [p. 16.31].

And when we read in the Ode that "the Son of Truth is
from the Most High Father" (l. 16) and that "the name of
the Father was on" the book, "and of the Son, and of the
Holy Ghost, to rule forever and ever," we think at once
of the discussion of the Son as the Father's Name in the
Gospel (pp. 38–40), and of the description of Truth as
the Father's Mouth and of the Spirit as the Father's Tongue
(p. 26.34–36).

Another important parallel occurs in Ode 38, where we
read how Truth became a haven of salvation to the writer;
it went with him and brought him to rest (ll. 3–4).

Error fled away from them and met them not,
  but the Truth proceeds in the right way.
Whatever I did not know, it showed me,
  all the poisons of Error and the plagues which pass for
    the fear of death and the destructive destroyer [ll. 6–7].
I asked the Truth, "Who are these?"
And he said to me, "This is the Deceiver and the Error"
  [ll.9–10]. . . .

Later on, salvation is described as the laying of a foundation, the planting of a root, and its springing up and bring-
ing forth fruit.

This too is the doctrine of the Gospel of Truth, where
Error is the foe of spiritual men. It elaborates matter in the
Void (p. 17.15) and made a creature in imitation of the

Truth (p. 17.19). Error annihilated Jesus (p. 18.24), but he showed men the right path; "that path is the Truth which he taught them" (p. 18.20). They find their true root, which is his root; and from other Valentinian documents we know that they bring forth fruit.

In the first edition of this book I followed the lead of several scholars who once suggested that the Odes are Valentinian. The resemblances remain striking, but as Daniélou has indicated one should also note the differences.[17] What the Odes have in common with the Gospel of Truth is a speculative Jewish Christianity which comes close to Gnosticism but is not fully Gnostic.

It seems significant that among the Church Fathers we find no real attempt to refute the Valentinian doctrine set forth in the Gospel of Truth or in the *Odes of Solomon;* indeed, the *Odes* were used in the worship of the Syrian church (though also in the Gnostic *Pistis Sophia*). The reason for this absence of polemic—of the *Gospel* Irenaeus says only that it is not like the canonical four [18]—presumably lies in its closeness to some other Christian teaching in the second century. Theologians who were willing to regard the *Shepherd of Hermas* as scripture could not easily attack the *Gospel of Truth.*

VALENTINIAN DEVELOPMENTS

But Valentinian theology, like its Christian counterparts, developed. And it developed in a direction away from what was becoming Christian orthodoxy. Either in the hands of Valentinus himself or of his disciple Ptolemaeus, it was "mythologized," and elements of the Syrian gnosis we have found in Saturninus and the Apocryphon of John entered the system. A decade ago, before the discovery of the *Gospel*, Quispel attempted to recover "the original doctrine of Valentine" by combining various passages in Irenaeus, Clement, and Hippolytus which differed from the Valentinian doctrine set forth, after Ptolemaeus, in the treatise of Irenaeus.[19] He no longer believes that this was the original doctrine, but it would appear that his reconstruction still possesses value as showing how either Valentinus or an early Valentinian developed the ideas found in the Gospel.

In this early system we find not one but two primal principles, Depth and Silence.[20] From these emanate Mind and Truth, then other pairs of aeons. Yet—and here we disagree with the Quispel of 1947—one of the two accounts which Irenaeus followed says that Valentinus spoke of one perfect aeon in the beginning, and that he called it both Depth and Father, or "the perfect Father." [21] This account, in agreement with the Gospel of Truth, must give Valentinus' original doctrine. Irenaeus also tells us that Sophia, last of the aeons, fell; out of her ignorance, sorrow, grief, and despair—equivalent to the error, anguish, oblivion, and terror of the Gospel of Truth—emerged the Creator. Nothing was said of such a Creator in the Gospel, where Error personified makes the creation. From this point the doctrine apparently developed toward mythology.

Again, in this form of Valentinianism it is said that spirit

arose out of Sophia's imaginative perception and was
secretly deposited in man; no trace of this doctrine oc-
curred in the Gospel, and it looks like an importation from
Saturninian-Ophite gnosis. The Christology of this system
is similar to that of the Gospel, with a few variants. Christ
comes down from above and enters into the spiritual human
being Jesus; he leaves Jesus at the crucifixion, but then
destroys death, raises up Jesus' mortal body, and carries
it above. He sits down at the right hand of the Creator in
order to provide the elect with a "way" into the Pleroma.
At present, spiritual beings "rest" in the intermediate place
with Sophia. Eventually they will put off their souls and,
with Christ's angels, will pass into the Pleroma, attaining
"the vision of the Father" and "the spiritual and eternal
mystery of sacred marriage."

This stage of Valentinian doctrine may come from Valentinus himself, but it is more highly mythologized than
the doctrine found in the Gospel of Truth. The genuine
and original doctrine certainly has mythological aspects,
but it is expressed more in abstract than in mythological
terms. It is also, we must remember, found in a gospel
presumably read in the Valentinian liturgy.

What differentiates Valentinian doctrine from Christian
is its mythological account of events in and just below the
Pleroma, and its notion of the ignorance of the creator.
Roman Gnosticism in general was at first relatively favor-
able toward the Creator. For instance, while Marcion
argued that the Creator was not good and was only just,
though he held that matter was evil, he was unwilling to

abandon the notion that he *was* just; it was Marcion's later disciples who called the Creator wicked.[22] While in the system of Theodotus the Creator is hostile toward the elect,[23] such a notion does not seem to be expressed by Valentinus himself or by Ptolemaeus. It seems to me that the development of Marcionite and Valentinian doctrine is the same; it develops in the direction of hostility toward the Creator.[24] Here it departs from Judaism and Christianity; as Hermas says, "the God of the powers . . . by his mighty power and his great wisdom created the world"; he is one, and he "made all things out of the nonexistent." [25] And while Hermas believes that the holy angels were created first, including six who were greater than the others, this fact is irrelevant, since the Creator made them all.[26]

Thus, the original doctrines of Marcion and Valentinus were relatively close to Christianity—and in the Gospel of Truth there is no mention of a Demiurge at all. But as they separated the world from God and spoke first of a Creator merely just or ignorant, they had to leave the community of Catholic Christians at Rome. Marcion was expelled; Valentinus may have withdrawn after failing to win an episcopal election. It became obvious that neither stood for the cardinal Christian doctrine of the unity of God and the goodness of his creation.

The Church Fathers were also disturbed by Gnostic ethics, which they regarded as lack of ethics. For instance, after Marcion had rejected the Old Testament law he was asked what curb he had left for sin. Tertullian tells us that he was accustomed to reply, "Absit, absit." [27] Such a reply seemed ridiculous to the Carthaginian Father. But it is nothing but a reiteration of the phrase Paul used under similar circumstances: μὴ γένοιτο ("By no means"). "Should we remain in sin, so that grace may abound? Μὴ γένοιτο" (Rom. 6.1–2). Marcion, like some Christians after him, was willing to keep the teaching of Jesus and Paul and abandon its Old Testament foundation.

On the other hand, some Valentinians came close to the doctrines of the licentious Gnostics we discussed in Chapter 3. They held that they were unharmed by what they did, just as gold is unharmed by mud. And they argued that while it is undoubtedly harmful for a merely psychic being (such as an orthodox Christian) to have intercourse with a woman, it is essential for a Valentinian to do so, since his action is an earthly symbol of the unions of the aeons above.[28] Not unnaturally, the Church Fathers were irritated by this teaching.

On these two grounds, therefore—the denial of the goodness of the Creator and the creation, and the lack of Jewish or Christian (or for that matter, Greco-Roman) moral teaching—the Church felt itself bound to expel both Marcion and Valentinus from its fellowship.

Valentinus himself seems to have moved away from the mystical Jewish Christian doctrine of the Gospel of Truth toward a more logical and mythological point of view. I have already suggested that he may have done so under the influence of his pupil Ptolemaeus, who was the great systematizer, apologist, and exegete of the Valentinian school.

Ptolemaeus was a systematizer: much of the first book of
Irenaeus' treatise against heresies is devoted to an exposition
of his system,[29] and Irenaeus himself indirectly owes much
to him.[30] Ptolemaeus was an apologist: we possess his *Letter
to Flora,* an attempt to persuade a Christian woman, or
church, that in Valentinianism she can find the true explanation of the inconsistencies of the Old Testament, and of
the truths of the New.[31] Ptolemaeus tries to lead "Flora"
down the garden path by showing her that she can avoid
Marcion by following Valentinus. Ptolemaeus was an exegete: much of the system is directly based on explanations
of more or less obscure passages in the New Testament.
Indeed, it can be claimed that the Valentinians were responsible for the rise of traditional Christian New Testament exegesis. Irenaeus and others were forced to look hard
at the New Testament, hard as they had never looked before. Two more Valentinian teachers profoundly influenced more orthodox exegetes. One was the "Oriental"
Valentinian Theodotus, whose ideas are known from the
excerpts made by Clement of Alexandria.[32] The other was
the Western or Italian Heracleon, who published exegetical
notes on the Gospel of John. These worried Origen so
much that he frequently quoted them in his own commentary. An allegorizer himself, Origen could not criticize
Heracleon's method—except by calling it "forced" or
"strained." [33] Both method and results influenced Origen.
   Valentinian exegesis disturbed ordinary Christians partly
because of the widespread acceptance of allegorical exegesis
in the Greco-Roman world. It was hard to prove that what

they said was in the New Testament wasn't there. More-over, since Valentinianism and earlier Christianity had a great deal in common, it was often necessary to revise Christian language in order to exclude Valentinian over-tones. One example will suffice.[34]

The followers of Ptolemaeus were willing to admit that the Christ was born in human fashion and had a real body; but this body was composed of psychic substance and was not "earthly" like ours; it had not come *from* Mary and had only passed *through* her.

This statement seems surprising, but the earlier orthodox Christian Justin had said nearly the same thing. To be sure, he had not mentioned "psychic substance," but he had al-most always said that Christ came "through" Mary; he had held that he was not a man like other men, and that his blood was produced not by man but by the power of God. All this language was at least ambiguous; at most it was Valentinian. It was necessary for Irenaeus to express the orthodox faith much more precisely.

Not only the language of earlier theologians, but also the language of the New Testament itself (especially the Paul-ine Epistles), could be pressed into Valentinian service. And while we may prefer to believe that the New Testament should be interpreted historically, especially in relation to its Jewish background, the Valentinians were by no means so timid. Like Marcion, they relied upon some of the less cautious statements of Paul and used them as keys for the understanding of the rest of his writings. It is obvious that their interpretation was heretical and that it led to schism. It is not so easy to prove that it was always wrong.

Both Valentinus and Marcion were deeply disturbing to the equilibrium of the Church Fathers because their systems were so closely related to Christianity, not because they were philosophical theologians. Marcion appealed to the apostle Paul and regarded the subsequent history of Christianity as a history of distortion and interpolation. The other apostles interpolated the pure Gospel by combining legalistic expressions with it. The Valentinians argued that, while the tradition was relatively pure, its purity was preserved only in stories of what Jesus did and said when he was alone with his disciples. To these disciples he also gave secret teaching which was handed down not in the Church's Gospels but in the Valentinian books.[35]

Because these Gnostic ideas were so disturbing, Christians like Justin, Theophilius, Irenaeus, and Tertullian had to devote a great deal of effort to showing that Marcionite and Valentinian presuppositions were not in harmony with the whole Bible, that is, both Old and New Testaments, or with the Christian traditions to which they themselves adhered. In a sense, the argument of these Christians was circular, and it would appear that they appealed, at times, to Greek philosophy, especially Middle Platonism, in order to gain further support for their claims. Moreover, they were forced by their opponents to construct a biblical theology, or theologies, in order to show that the main lines of biblical thought were opposed to Gnosticism. They also proceeded

to attack the morality of the Gnostics and thus were led
toward a kind of legalism which Paul, at least, would have
found un-Christian.

In other words, the systems of Marcion and Valentinus
were largely Christian in origin. Some Church writers recognized this when they said Marcion's father was a bishop
in Pontus and that Valentinus nearly became a bishop himself.[36]

BASILIDES

We have seen that Valentinianism is a theological process
not unlike orthodox Christianity itself. It contains mythological and philosophical elements, but it cannot be used
to demonstrate the theory that gnosis begins with myth
and ends with philosophical theology. Moreover, we have
observed the diversity present in the thought of various
Valentinian teachers. This diversity means that we cannot speak of Valentinian gnosis without specifying the
kind of Valentinianism we mean.

Perhaps a better example of a trend from myth to philosophy will be provided by the Alexandrian Gnostic teacher
Basilides, who flourished during the reign of Hadrian (117–
138). A measure of confusion is provided by the accounts
given by Irenaeus and Hippolytus regarding Basilides' doctrine, for the systems they describe are quite different from
each other. Modern scholars generally agree, however, that
Irenaeus has perhaps described a later development, as he

does in dealing with Valentinianism; the authentic Basilidian system is that described by Hippolytus.[37]

There was a time when there was nothing, but "nothing" was not anything existent. Simply and plainly, without any sophistry, there was absolutely nothing. When I say "was," I do not mean that anything was; I use the word in order to signify what I want to indicate—I mean that there was absolutely nothing. . . . Since, then, there was nothing—no matter, no substance, no non-substance, nothing simple, nothing complex, nothing not understood, nothing not sensed, no man, no angel, no god, not any thing that is named or perceived through sense or any intelligible things, and not anything which can be defined as more subtle than anything else: the non-existent God wished (without intelligence, without sense, without will, without choice, without passion, without desire) to make a cosmos. I say he "wished" for the sake of saying something; but it was without wish, without intelligence, without sense; and "cosmos" is not the one with breadth and divisibility, which came into existence later, and remained in existence, but the seed of the cosmos. . . . So the non-existent God made a non-existent cosmos out of the non-existent.

This is the most extreme statement of the illusory nature of God and of the universe which has been set forth by any Gnostic, ancient or modern. It has philosophical overtones; the language Basilides uses is characteristic of Greek philosophy. But the striking thing about the statement is that Basilides himself regarded it as an explanation of one verse in Genesis (1.3: "Let there be light") and another in John (1.9: "It was the true light"). Moreover, it is a philosophically respectable variant of the unrespectable doctrine

held by Jews and Christians in Basilides' time. The schools
agreed that "nothing is produced out of nothing, even by
divine power." [38] But the common Christian teaching is
that set forth by Hermas in his first mandate: "First of all,
believe that God is one, who founded and finished all
things, and made all things for existence, out of the non-
existent." In Hermas' statement there are two existents,
God and all things, and one nonexistent, the substance God
used. In ordinary philosophical teaching there are three
existents: God, all things, and the substance. Basilides holds
firmly that the universe was made *ex nihilo*, and he main-
tains his doctrine by asserting the nonexistence of God, all
things, and the substance God used.

Professor Wolfson has recently drawn the attention of
scholars to another passage where Basilides is thinking along
philosophical lines.[39] Basilides says that God cannot be described even as ineffable (as Philo described him); "that
which is named [ineffable] is not absolutely ineffable, since
we call one thing ineffable and another not even ineffable.
For that which is not even ineffable is not named ineffable,
but is above every name that is named." [40] In Basilides' view
the expression "God is ineffable" is a mere privation, im-
plying that by his nature God could be effable. He wants
to express his doctrine still more negatively.

But does this doctrine, in which, as Wolfson has shown,
Basilides is dealing with Aristotelian teaching, make Basilides a philosopher? On the contrary, it seems to me that Basilides' starting point is not in philosophy but in exegesis.
The expression "above every name that is named" comes

from Ephesians 1.21, where it is used to describe the height to which God has raised Christ. With this passage we may compare Philippians 2.9, which says that God gave the risen Christ "the name which is above every name." But if God is above such an ineffable height and can give such an ineffable name, obviously he himself must be beyond ineffability. A similar doctrine, likewise based on the Philippians passage,[41] is found in the Valentinian Gospel of Truth, where we read that the Father's Name "does not belong to the [category of] words or to the [category of] appellations . . . for indeed the Unengendered has no name." [42] Philosophical language was used by Basilides and by Valentinus alike, but neither of them was a philosopher.

According to Basilides the history of the universe was roughly as follows. What the nonexistent god made was a nonexistent seed, the seed of the cosmos. It did not emanate from him as if he were a spider; he made it. Now in this seed was a "tripartite Sonship"; one part was subtle, another opaque, a third in need of purification. The first Sonship at once returned to the nonexistent god. The second Sonship also returned to the nonexistent god, but left behind its "wing," the Holy Spirit, set as a kind of "firmament" between the hypercosmic world and the cosmos. The third Sonship remained in the seed. Then from the seed was produced the great Archon who created the cosmos out of materials available in the seed; he also begot a son and seated him at his right hand. After this, another Archon arose and made this world and also begot a son; this Archon was the god of Abraham, Isaac, and Jacob.

Still later, the light of the Gospel came down from the Sonship above, through both Archons, who then realized that they were not supreme gods, and it came upon Jesus, the son of Mary. The lowest Sonship is being refashioned and is following Jesus upward and is going above the firmament to the nonexistent god. Jesus is working out the distinction between psychic beings and spiritual beings. Spiritual beings, the "men of the Sonship," return above. When they have all returned, the nonexistent god will bring about cosmic ignorance for the rest, including the Archons below the firmament.

Is this doctrine philosophical? Some scholars have argued that it comes from Indian philosophy.[43] It is certainly possible that at Alexandria Basilides could have acquired some knowledge of Buddhism from Indian merchants and traders. But we have already argued that his doctrine of creation can be explained in relation to Greek philosophy, and Quispel has shown that there are Middle Platonist roots for the notion of the "tripartite Sonship."[44] We therefore find it unnecessary to go so far afield as India. Should we go symbolically to Athens?

It seems, on the contrary, that while there are certainly philosophical elements in Basilides' thought, we must remember that its center lies in a myth which, according to his opponents, he claimed to have received by secret tradition from the apostle Peter.[45] And his personal attitude toward reality—what might be called a drive toward *Nichtigkeit*—was not philosophical. It is expressed in his pessimistic eschatology. At the end, everything here below will return to a state of cosmic oblivion. Those who remain below not only will not be saved but will be quite unaware of their need for salvation. This idea reminds us of the question in the Gospel: "When the Son of Man comes, will he find faith on the earth?" (Luke 18.8). This question is surprising in the Gospel, but it is characteristic of the system of Basilides.

Terms and ideas in the system have been borrowed from Greek philosophy. They led Hippolytus astray so that he treated Basilides as an Aristotelian philosopher. Hippolytus' analysis was wrong, for like Saturninus of Antioch Basilides was primarily concerned with man's hopeless state here on earth and with the possibility of salvation offered by Jesus.

PHILOSOPHICAL GNOSTICISM

We have tried to argue that not even Basilides can be characterized as a philosopher, and that Gnosticism is not a form of philosophy. What, then, are we to say when we encounter Gnostic-like notions in more clearly philosophical writings? The writings we have in mind are the fragments of the philosopher Numenius of Apamea, the *Chaldaean Oracles* and the Hermetic treatises and fragments. Martin Nilsson, for example, has argued that the *Hermetica* represent pagan gnosis, while what we have previously discussed is Christian gnosis.[46]

It is a real question whether Numenius should be regarded as Gnostic except in a peripheral way. Rudolf Beutler has provided good grounds for treating Numenius' thought within the framework of Middle Platonism; [47] and the possible influence of Oriental theologies on him does not make him a Gnostic.[48] "It would appear," says Beutler, "that Numenius interpreted Oriental teaching, especially Jewish Christian, in a Platonic manner."

Again, the teaching of the *Chaldaean Oracles*, late in the second century, consists, as Nilsson has pointed out, of a "semiphilosophical dress for a theurgy which originates in mysteries and fire-rites." [49] There are strong resemblances to Gnostic ideas. Everything emanates from the supreme Father, known only by revelation, who helps the soul or divine spark in its struggle against the body. His angels help the soul remember its divine origin and escape upwards to unite with him.[50]

As for the *Hermetica*, Festugière has insisted upon the eclectic Middle Platonic character of these documents.[51] They come out of a milieu of popular philosophy, not from the mythological Gnosis we have previously discussed. I should agree with van Moorsel that the *Hermetica* are not Gnostic. They know no savior, and they are only slightly dualistic; saving gnosis is not exclusively knowledge of the self, but is knowledge of the world as well.[52] But since no one view is consistently maintained throughout the writings, I should be willing to use the term "gnosticizing" employed by Quispel, or "semi-Gnosticism" as suggested by van Moorsel.[53]

It is difficult to classify the systems we have just mentioned. Somehow they stand on the borderline between

the pure Gnosticism we have encountered elsewhere and
the philosophies from which they borrow so much.

Daniélou has pointed out that one should note the differences among these systems. The *Chaldaean Oracles* owe
nothing to Judaism or Christianity; Numenius was inter-
ested in them only as providing illustrations for a system
built on other foundations; only in some of the Hermetic
writings is there clear evidence of speculations on Genesis.
Origen tells us that Numenius alluded to Jesus—but without mentioning his name.[54]

Those Gnostics who were closest to Christianity also
tended to argue that their system was authentic and original
Christianity. Marcion's system was the teaching of Jesus
and Paul, freed from the interpolations made by Judaizers.
The teachings of Valentinus and Basilides were said to have
been handed down to them by disciples of Paul and Peter.
It is easy enough for us to state that these ideas are wrong.
Gnostic Christianity, we are likely to say, is not Christianity at all. But it is an interesting question whether the teaching of the Gospels and of the Epistles is more adequately
reinterpreted by these Gnostic teachers or by such second-
century "orthodox" teachers as the apologists and Irenaeus.
The answer given this question by the Church, in the
second century and after, was obviously the rejection of
Gnosticism. Even the "Christian Gnosticism" of Clement
and Origen was suspect. Clement was never canonized, and
Origen was condemned in 551. Perhaps for us to give an
answer would require a definition of an "adequate reinterpretation"; and this lies beyond the scope of these lectures.

It is worth noting, however, that when Celsus wrote his attack on Christianity, in the reign of Marcus Aurelius, he found Christianity just as unpalatable as Gnosticism; and this attitude recurs in Plotinus and Porphyry.

Ultimately, the difference between Christian and Gnostic philosophical theology seems to lie in their attitudes toward the world. For any Gnostic the world is really hell. For Christians the world is one which God made, a world whose history he governs.

6

GNOSTICISM AND
EARLY CHRISTIANITY

WE HAVE now seen something of the ways in which the principal early Gnostic systems were developed, and in which at least the Valentinians endeavored to come closer to the "Great Church." From time to time we have indicated some of the striking parallels to be found between Gnostic ideas and statements made in the New Testament. But now we must proceed to investigate the relation of early Christianity to Gnosticism and to the sources of Gnosticism in Jewish apocalyptic thought and in other kinds of Jewish speculation. From the previous chapters it will be evident that we shall encounter difficulties; for if something in the New Testament resembles Gnostic expressions, it is likely to resemble expressions found in Jewish apocalyptic or haggada, and we may not be able to state precisely what its origins are.

JESUS

In the Synoptic Gospels we find almost nothing which seems to be related to Gnosticism, even though, as we have

seen, some Gnostics were able to find support for their
views by allegorical interpretation of the sayings of Jesus
or, at times, by noncontextual literal exegesis. There are
two passages, however, in which a kind of semi-Gnostic
language occurs. The first is found in both Matthew
(11.25–27) and Luke (10.21–22).

I praise thee, Father, Lord of heaven and earth, because thou
hast hidden these things from the wise and understanding, and
hast revealed them to infants; yea, Father, for so it was well
pleasing before thee. All things have been delivered to me by
my Father, and no one knows the Son but the Father, nor
does anyone know the Father but the Son and whoever receives
the revelation from the Son.

This passage presents the Son as the sole organ of revelation,
and as B. W. Bacon argued long ago, it is based on the picture of Israel in Jewish speculation.[1] Norden called the
language "mystical-theosophical"; [2] more recently, W. D.
Davies has claimed that it is apocalyptic.[3] Actually it is
both. It stands on the borderline between apocalyptic and
Gnostic thought, and does so in the context of Jewish
speculation about the Israel, the Torah, and the Wisdom
of God. And it obviously points onward toward the Fourth
Gospel, where we read that "the Father loves the Son and
has given all things into his hand" (John 3.35), that "the
Father knows me and I know the Father" (10.15), and
that "no one comes to the Father but by me" (14.6).

The second passage occurs in Matthew alone (11.28–30).

Come to me, all who labor and are burdened, and I will refresh
you. Take my yoke upon you and learn from me, for I am

meek and lowly of heart, and you will find rest for your souls; for my yoke is easy and my burden is light.

Here again the thought is related to ideas about the Wisdom or the Torah of God. A prayer of Jesus son of Sirach begins with the words, "I praise thee, Lord King" (51.1) and ends with an appeal based on his own experience. "Draw near to me, you who are untaught. . . . Put your neck under the yoke [of Wisdom] and let your souls receive instruction; it is to be found close by. . . . I have found for myself much rest" (51.23–27). Wisdom is the "close-by" Torah of God, as in Sirach 51.26 (Bar. 3.29); and she has "tabernacled" in Jacob and in Israel (24.8). But in this passage in Matthew we do not hear about Wisdom from Jesus son of Sirach; we hear the words of Jesus the Wisdom of God. There is a Wisdom-Christology in this passage which points toward the Gnostic speculations about Wisdom. But here it is not Gnostic; it is simply Christian, and it may go back to Jesus himself. If Jesus somehow identified himself with Israel, as many modern scholars have held, it is surely possible that he could have identified himself with the Wisdom of God. In any event, we can see that at a very early time he was so identified by Christians.

It is obvious that the picture of Jesus which is reflected in these sayings does not easily blend with the portrait of him as an enthusiast for apocalyptic eschatology which is widely accepted by New Testament critics today. On the other hand, significant protests against the current view have been raised by such scholars as C. H. Dodd, J. A. T.

Robinson, and E. Stauffer. Dodd argued in favor of "real-ized eschatology" or "eschatology in process of realiza-tion"; [4] Robinson examined the whole synoptic tradition in order to show that the more apocalyptic-eschatological doctrines were added by early Christians to the teaching of Jesus; [5] and Stauffer has pointed out that in the com-mon source of Matthew and Luke (in which we find the first passage discussed above) there is no mention whatever of an imminent end of the world. "The tendency of the community," writes Stauffer, "to add oracular utterances about the imminent end of the world is most clearly evi-dent in the tradition of the Gospel of Matthew, which originated in the apocalyptic years shortly before the catas-trophic fall of Jerusalem." [6] This date for Matthew may be too early, but it is undeniable that the tradition he sets forth has been set in a framework in which apocalyptic eschatology has been heightened.

If the mission of Jesus was not purely, or even primarily, eschatological in nature—except in so far as it represented the fulfillment of eschatological hopes—then we can more easily understand how the interpretations of his person provided by Paul (except in Thessalonians), by John, and by various Gnostic teachers could arise. Apocalyptic escha-tologists interpreted him in one way; others, with greater reliance on Jewish Wisdom conceptions and on Jewish speculations about the Word and the Name of God, and perhaps on his own teaching, interpreted him in another.

PAUL

It may be that we can find traces of Gnostic ideas in the letters of Paul, although to find out what Paul thought and how and why he thought it is more difficult than might at first appear. We do not really know a great deal about the circumstances under which he wrote his letters, and to a considerable extent the circumstances have to be inferred from the letters themselves. Some scholars have tried to trace a development in his thought and to explain it partly on psychological grounds; [7] others have claimed that development cannot be traced [8] and that as an apologist for the gospel he really tried, as he says, to become "all things to all men" (1 Cor. 9.22).[9] With or without a theory of development, however, it is fairly plain that the atmosphere of such early letters as those to the Thessalonians is more apocalyptic-eschatological than that of such a letter as Romans, not to mention Colossians and Ephesians. Only in 2 Thessalonians (2.2) do we hear of converts who believe that "the day of the Lord has arrived."

We shall examine the Pauline Epistles by beginning with Thessalonians and then going on via Corinthians to the letters to the Colossians and Ephesians. Finally, we shall deal with the Pastoral Epistles, which almost certainly represent "post-Pauline Paulinism."

In what are probably Paul's earliest letters, those to the Thessalonians, there are no traces whatever of anything resembling Gnostic doctrine. Instead, there is a vigorous and rather crude apocalyptic eschatology; the Lord is going to come down from heaven and we shall meet him in the air (1 Thess. 4.16–17). The Lord Jesus will appear with the angels of his power, with the fire of a flame (2 Thess. 1.7–8).

In Galatians, however, something a little different occurs. Paul tells his converts not to serve gods who are not really gods, the "weak and impoverished *stoicheia*." They once served them when they observed a calendar which included "days, months, seasons, and years" (Gal. 4.8–10). Who can these *stoicheia* be but the planetary spirits, weak and impoverished because somehow Christ has triumphed over them? And it may be—though caution is certainly necessary—that they are to be identified with the angels through whom, Paul says (Gal. 3.19), the Mosaic law was ordained.[10] Paul's doctrine is not by any means Gnostic; it is apocalyptic but it is coming closer to Gnosticism.

It is worth noting that in this letter Paul's emphasis is shifting from the future to what Christ has already done. He has rescued us from the present evil age (1.4); it is no longer Paul who lives, but Christ who lives in him (2.20); the world has been crucified to him, and he to the world (6.14); a new creation has already come (6.15).

This doctrine is no different from what we later meet in Colossians, where we learn that we have "died with Christ and are separated from the *stoicheia* of the world" (2.20). Our true life is now a hidden life, hidden with Christ in God (3.3).

The Corinthian letters have been regarded, especially in recent times, as evidence for the existence of Gnostic sectarianism in the Christian community. Though the ability of modern scholars to recover Paul's opponents' ideas may be over-estimated, it would appear that a movement like the one which later became Gnosticism was probably present in Corinth.[11] The framework in which the Corinthians expressed many of their ideas about themselves was derived from the Cynic-Stoic ideal "wise man," who was regarded as "powerful," "well-born" (1 Cor. 1:26), "rich," and "royal"(4:8). He lived in accordance with nature and therefore matters of diet and of sexual activity were "indifferent" as far as he was concerned; again, everything and anything was "permissible" for him, as it was to a king (cf. 6:12–13). But why did these Corinthians hold such a view of themselves? It would appear that two features of Christian life were especially influential in the development of their ideas. (1) There was the experience of the activity of the Spirit within the community; in their view, the gift of the Spirit made them "spiritual." (2) There was the proclamation of the imminent kingdom of God; in their view, this kingdom had already come, and therefore they were "filled" and "rich"; since the kingdom was theirs, they were kings (cf. the Sermon on the Mount). In other words, in place of an eschatology in process of realization the Corinthian sectarians had a fully-realized eschatology, which they interpreted in semi-philosophical terms. They may have laid special emphasis on the conception of Jesus as the Wisdom of God (cf. 1:18–2:5).

It is not so clear, however, that the Gnosticizing tendency present among them involved their setting forth a Gnosticizing or Gnostic myth. In a system much like theirs, that of Prodicus as described by Clement of Alexandria,[12] there is such a myth, describing the emanation of "the Beloved" from the primordial One. But all we know about myth at Corinth comes from what Paul sets forth of his own belief. He speaks of the mysterious "archons of this aeon" who are passing away and says that they crucified "the Lord of glory" because they did not know God's hidden wisdom (2:6-8). Chief among them was probably the one whom Paul calls "the god of this age" (2 Cor. 4:4). But is his language, or any of theirs which he may conceivably reflect, actually Gnostic? The term "the Lord of glory" occurs eight times in the apocalyptic book of Enoch, where it is used of God; the absolute distinctions Paul sets forth between Christ and Beliar and between light and darkness (2 Cor. 6:14-15) are close to the apocalyptic of the Dead Sea Scrolls—indeed, so close that some critics have suggested that 2 Corinthians 6:14-7:1 is not Paul's but a Dead Sea fragment. And in trying to determine the background of Paul's thought in both Corinthian letters we must recall that the legends to which he may refer in 2 Corinthians II (seduction of Eve by the serpent; Satan's transformation into an angel of light) occur in apocalyptic literature related to Adam, while the idea of rapture into the third heaven or into paradise (2 Cor. 12:2-4) is also characteristic of apocalyptic literature.[13]

It is true that such notions appear again among the Gnostics, but it need not be held that Paul himself has gone beyond apocalyptic toward, or into, Gnosticism. His interpretation of the Gospel in apocalyptic terminology, however, may have encouraged converts whose acquaintance with Judaism was minimal to understand him in a semi-Gnostic manner. Such a development may help us to explain the situation which probably underlies his letter to the Colossians.

As far as one can tell—and certainly some of this analysis has to be guesswork—the Colossians believed that there was a pleroma or fullness of divine being which was made up of the "elemental spirits of the world," the angels. They worshiped these angels and held that they themselves were bound to obey not only the Jewish law, which the angels had given, but also certain ascetic requirements (2.16, 21). This doctrine, which seems essentially Jewish in origin, they may have called by the name of "philosophy" (2.8). They may also have spoken of a special kind of knowledge (*epignosis*) of God (1.9–10; 2.2).[14]

It is doubtful that they were really dualists. When Paul tells them that God "delivered us from the power of darkness" he may well be expressing his own view, not theirs (1.13). In any case, he answers them by telling them that the "fulness of deity" was in Christ, not in these angels, and that every cosmic power was created in him—"thrones, dominations, principalities, powers" (1.16). God "blotted out the decree in ordinances which was against us, and took it from our midst, nailing it to the cross; he 'put off' the principalities and powers and made a public example of them, triumphing over them by him" (2.14–15). Paul's language is no less mythological than the Colossians', but it is centered in God and Christ, not in the angelic rulers.

What is Paul doing as he writes to the Colossians? He is correcting their rather simple, though speculative, angelology by insisting on his own "realized echatology." In the course of the development of his own thought from the Thessalonian epistles to this point, he has come to lay more and more emphasis on the realization of eschatology and to think less and less of the future coming of Jesus. The Christian is one who "has been raised with Christ" (3.1). Paul believes that Christ will be made manifest (3.4), but the center of emphasis has been shifted from future to past and present.

The Colossians actually seem to have been less dualistic than Paul himself. Perhaps this lack of dualism was due to a lack of concern for apocalyptic eschatology. In any event, their ideas—as far as we can recover them—cannot be used to prove the presence of Gnostic thinking in the Church when Colossians was written. Paul himself is moving in the direction of Gnosticism. We do not know that the Colossians were doing so.

The movement toward Gnosticism is almost completed by the time we reach the epistle to the Ephesians, for which the Gnostic background has been worked out by Heinrich Schlier.[15] It is hard to prove that Ephesians was written after the death of Paul and the fall of the temple, though modern studies have made such a theory fairly probable.[16] The mysterious reference in Ephesians 2.14 to the broken dividing wall between Jews and gentiles may suggest that the temple has been destroyed, though this is of course highly uncertain. In any case we are close to gnosis. Christians already live in the heavenly regions; the Church has already ascended to heaven in order to make the wisdom of God known to the principalities and powers. "Our warfare," says the author, "is against the principalities, against the powers, against the world-rulers of this darkness, against the spiritual beings of wickedness in the heavenly regions" (6.12). These spiritual beings are almost certainly planetary angels, and we agree with Schlier that the background of Ephesians lies in an incipient Gnosticism.

This is one answer which the Christian Church gives to the problem presented by the collapse of apocalyptic eschatology. In Ephesians the expectations set forth in the earliest Pauline Epistles are almost entirely transformed into cosmological doctrine. And if Ephesians was intended as a guide to reading Paul, we can see that it sets the other letters in a post- or non-apocalyptic perspective.

Still later, further reinterpretation was necessary. Genuine Gnostics were "twisting" the letters of Paul in favor of their systems (2 Pet. 3.15–16). And as we have already intimated, there was a good deal of material available for them to twist. For this reason an ecclesiastical author made the effort to provide an authoritative treatment of Paul's views. The Pastoral Epistles attack "myths and genealogies" (1 Tim. 1.4) or "Jewish myths" (Tit. 1.14), which may well be Gnostic accounts of the origin of the universe. They urge readers to "guard the deposit, avoiding the profane babblings and contradictions of the gnosis which is falsely so-called" (1 Tim. 6.20). And they oppose a gnosis which forbids marriage and requires abstinence from meat (1 Tim. 4.3). "Everything created by God is good" (1 Tim. 4.4). Surely those Church Fathers were right who believed that in these letters the Gnostic systems of the late first or early second century were under fire.

THE GOSPELS

The Church not only reinterpreted Paul but also continued its work of reinterpreting Jesus. In Matthew, for example, we find the retention and even the strengthening of apocalyptic eschatology. We also find the doctrine that Jesus proclaimed a new law to his disciples, the law of the kingdom of God.[17] Other evangelists, however, diminished the emphasis on eschatology.

In the first place, we find in Luke a reinterpretation of the units of oral tradition which were available to him, as well as (to some extent) of the whole gospel story. As Conzelmann suggests, he treats as historical what in Matthew, and to a lesser degree in Mark, is regarded as eschatological.[18] This means that he can say of the disciples that "they supposed that the kingdom of God was going to appear immediately" (19.11) and can recognize that they did not understand what they meant. Thus, Luke recognizes the distance between himself and some members, at least, of the primitive community. His own view of the kingdom is presumably that represented by the saying, "The kingdom of God is within you" or "in your possession" (17.21).[19] It is by no means clear, however, that this emphasis is due to the fall of Jerusalem, for as C. H. Dodd has pointed out, where Mark and Matthew describe this event in terms which recall the Maccabean struggle, Luke uses language borrowed from descriptions of the fall of Jerusalem in 586 B.C.[20]

An important problem related to Luke's de-emphasizing of apocalyptic eschatology is that of his historical accuracy. Does he "de-eschatologize" simply because historical events have taught him the advisability of doing so? Or is he relying on authentic materials, going back to the early Church in Jerusalem, in which it was clear that Jesus' mission was not so closely related to apocalyptic eschatology as it is in other gospels? Some of the considerations we have mentioned suggest that we should not hastily accept the first alternative. When Luke separates Christianity from Jewish apocalyptic movements [21] and possibly from Gnosticism [22] he may have good historical grounds for doing so.

Another kind of interpretation is given in the Gospel of John. With regard to this book, critical opinions have been characterized by a good deal of ebb and flow. In the nineteenth century it was fairly fashionable to date this Gospel in the middle, or even in the latter half, of the second century. The discovery of a papyrus fragment from the first half of the second century [23] and the growing recognition that John was used certainly in the Gospel of Truth, probably in the letters of Ignatius,[24] and quite possibly in 1 Clement [25] have increased the cautiousness of scholars, as has greater awareness of the diversity of theological outlooks within early Christianity. Against too early a date there remains the almost complete consensus of the Fathers that John's was chronologically the Fourth Gospel, though various scholars have argued that in his work there are reflections of synoptic tradition but not of the Synoptic Gospels.[26]

The Gospel is certainly the product of meditative reflection, but unfortunately such reflection is hard to measure in chronological terms. We already know that in synoptic tradition from a date at least relatively early there was consideration of Jesus as the Son and as the Wisdom of God. And it is this kind of speculation, as we shall see, which is reflected in John. It is difficult to tell whether the temple is still standing or not. John is concerned with the temple, the festivals, even with Palestinian geography; but both Josephus and the compilers of the Mishnah speak of the temple as if it were still standing and of the festivals as if they were being observed. We might find a clue in his references to "the Jews" as the enemies of Jesus were it not that at Qumran the "sons of Israel" are regarded as dominated by Belial.

Finally, it is a question how much the ecclesiastical tradition owes to its erroneous identification of the author of the Gospel with that of the Apocalypse; it may be this identification, questioned as early as the third century, which has put the Fourth Gospel late.

For these reasons we should not attempt to discuss the Gospel in relation to chronology but should instead endeavor to find out what kind of thought is represented in it. We cannot exclude the possibility that many of the sayings of Jesus found in it are actually interpretations of words actually spoken by him, though we must remember that the evangelist, whose memory, as he believed (John 14.26), was guided by the Spirit, has recast the sayings in his own style. And the differences between John and the synoptics cannot be overlooked. For John, Jesus is not the relatively human figure we encounter in the synoptics; his opponents are not so much persons as types. Other differences are harder to assess. When entrance into the kingdom of God becomes a matter of rebirth, birth from above, birth from water and Spirit (3.3–5), we cannot be sure that this conception is entirely alien to the teaching of Jesus. When resurrection at the last day is combined with participation in eternal life here and now, we cannot be certain that Jesus' preaching was exclusively limited to the former doctrine.

On the other hand, when Bultmann treats the synoptic-like passages as interpolations due to an ecclesiastical redactor, we cannot be sure that John did not mean to include them himself. He may have been less consistent, or "thorough-going," than critics could wish he had been. Indeed, he may have been trying to interpret the mission of Jesus, at least in part, in terms comprehensible to the sectarians of Qumran, for it is in the Johannine writings that we find some of the most striking parallels between the Scrolls and the New Testament. There, as K. G. Kuhn first pointed out, we find the contrasts between light and darkness, truth and falsehood, the sons of light under God and the sons of darkness under the world and the devil. There we find the notion of salvation by overcoming the world (though it is hard to find Christian writings which lie close to the War Scroll) and the eschatological community which lives in the world.[27]

It is almost certainly correct to say that the Dead Sea Scrolls cast significant light on the origins of the Fourth Gospel. It is almost certainly incorrect to claim that they,

and they alone, are responsible for the form or "shape" of
Johannine thought. Scholars not obsessed by novelty can
still recognize the relevance of the various elements in the
mosaic of Johannine theology—for example, the influence
of something like the thought of Philo,[28] the influence of
rabbinic Judaism,[29] and even the forms of expression, at
least, to be found in the *Hermetica* and in Gnosticism.[30]
The difference between John and the Qumran sectarians
can perhaps be seen in the prologue with which the Gospel
begins.

The key to the Gospel of John, at any rate in the form in
which we possess it, is provided by its poetic, hymnodic
prologue (1.1–18). Most scholars agree that in order to
link the prologue with what he is about to say of John the
Baptist, the evangelist has inserted remarks about the Baptist into the prologue (1.6–8, 15). The rest of the prologue
is a poem of creation and salvation.

In the beginning was the Word, and the Word was with God,
And the Word was God, this which was in the beginning with
 God.
Everything came into existence through It,
And apart from It nothing came into existence.
What came into existence in It was life,
And the life was the light of men.
The light shines in the darkness, and the darkness did not
 grasp It.
It was the true light, which illuminates every man;
It was coming into the world.
It was in the world, and the world came into existence
 through It,
And the world did not know It.
It came to Its own, and Its own did not receive It.

But those who did receive It,
To them It gave the power to become children of God—
Those who believe in His Name,
Those who were begotten, not from human nature
(Or from the will of the flesh or from the will of a man)
But from God.
And the Word became flesh and dwelt among us,
And we beheld Its glory, glory as of an Only-begotten from
  the Father,
(Full of grace and truth).
For from His Fulness have we all received grace after grace.
No one has ever seen God;
The Only-begotten, who is in the Father's bosom,
It made Him known.

It is hard to translate the pronouns which refer to the Logos. In English, "he" is both masculine and personal, while "it" is neuter and impersonal. John is speaking of a power of God which (or who) becomes incarnate, so to speak, only in the 18th verse of the prologue. We shall try to solve the problem by capitalizing *It*.

A greater difficulty is presented by "Logos" itself. What does it mean? Word, matter, reason, thought, or deed? This question can be answered only by finding out what the whole prologue is about. One answer to what it is about has been given by scholars who have noticed that everything said about the Logos in the prologue is said about the heavenly Wisdom in late Jewish literature.[31] This observation gives a partial solution. But John does not speak of God's Wisdom; he speaks of God's Logos. And if we look at Sirach 24.3, we find Wisdom as Word saying, "I came forth from the mouth of the Most High." Furthermore, we know that in the book of Genesis (which John is clearly imitating when he says, "In the beginning") creation takes place when Elohim says a word: "Let there be." The most natural solution for Logos is the traditional one: translate it by "word," the creative word of God often mentioned in the Old Testament.

But if we try to go on reading John's prologue in the manner of a speculative, haggada-minded Jewish exegete we may find further levels of meaning in it. When Elohim said y^ehi '$\bar{o}r$, "let there be light," he was uttering the name Yahweh, for in Exodus 3.14 we read that the name YHWH is derived from the verb HWH, "to be." The word of God is therefore the name of God, and when John says that "nothing came into existence apart from It" he means that God spoke creative words and that the essence of each creative word was his name. "What came into existence in It was life," since $hayah$ resembles both YHWH and HWH; "and the life was light"—as it says in Genesis.

In other words, the prologue of the Fourth Gospel may begin with a complex midrashic speculation on the opening verses of Genesis. Such speculations occur elsewhere in the New Testament. The best example is to be found in Colossians 1.15–20, where Paul is working over texts taken from Genesis and Proverbs.[32]

And this speculative element is not absent from the rest of the Gospel, as modern commentators have made plain.[33] The "I am" sayings found in John can sometimes be paralleled in Greco-Roman aretalogies of gods and goddesses; but their source lies in the explanation of the name Yahweh which is provided in Exodus. The Father has given Jesus his own name (John 17.11), and it is for this reason that

Jesus can say that he and the Father are one (10.30). The Father is still creatively working, and Jesus is creatively working too (5.17). And all this can be known from the writings of Moses—in other words, from the Pentateuch—for Moses wrote about the incarnate word (5.46). Where did he write? Presumably in the creation story of Genesis, and in the explanation of God's name in Exodus, and in other places as well.

The kind of speculation we find in John is what we find a little later in the Gospel of Truth. It is like that gospel and like the equally Valentinian *Odes of Solomon*. It is indubitably Jewish, but it is on the verge of Gnosticism.

The expression "Its own did not receive It" shows us plainly that we are not dealing with a Gnostic hymn or poem. For a Gnostic, the power from above could have come only to be received by its own, even though the way to recognize oneself as belonging to the power from above would be by receiving it. Therefore, we are in a somewhat different atmosphere, and this atmosphere can only be that of Judaism, where the story of Israel is the story of God's dealings with a rebellious people which often rejects his messengers and kills his prophets. The Jews rejected Jesus, says the Christian author, yet they were *his* own; for "salvation originates with the Jews" (John 4.22).[34]

Similarly, the statement that the Word "dwelt" or "tabernacled" among us is not surprising in a Jewish hymn related to the heavenly Wisdom, for in Sirach 24.13 we hear the Creator say to Sophia, "Tabernacle in Jacob and be an inheritance in Israel."[35] The hymn could even be used by a Jewish Gnostic, were it not for the crucial sentence,

"And the Word became flesh." [36] This means that the divine creative Word, Wisdom, Name of God became a human being. Nothing could be more clearly un-Gnostic, or even anti-Gnostic. For it is an essential part of Gnostic theory to insist either that the divine Christ was not human or that the divine Christ descended upon the human Jesus. John says, "The Word *became* flesh."

The background of this part of the prologue lies in Psalm 84(85).9–10.

> God's salvation is near to those who fear him,
> So that glory may tabernacle in our land.
> Grace and truth have met together;
> Righteousness has descended from heaven.

How has righteousness descended from heaven? In the person of the incarnate Only-begotten, who alone has revealed God to men.

And the men who received him became like the patriarchs Isaac and Jacob; they were begotten in no ordinary human way, "but of God," as we read in the Old Testament (Gen. 21.1; 25.21). Before John's time, the Jew Philo had speculated on the significance of the "virginal conceptions" of Sarah and Rebecca, and John himself tells us that "your father Abraham rejoiced" to see the day of Jesus (8.56). How does he know that Abraham rejoiced? He has read in Genesis 17.17 that Abraham rejoiced when he heard God's promise of the birth of Isaac.[37] Once more, we are in the atmosphere of Jewish speculation on the hidden meaning of the Old Testament. Yet the Judaism has been Christianized. For John, being born of God is not simply a matter related to the patriarchs. It is something which happens to the believer when he is "born again," when he is "begotten of water and Spirit" (3.5).[38] A Gnostic could say this, but he could say it only if he had encountered Christian baptism.

Two themes which occur frequently in the course of the Gospel reveal some relationship to Gnostic ways of thinking. One is the theme of the direction of human existence and of the life of the incarnate Word. Human beings know nothing about this direction. They do not know whence the wind (or the Spirit) comes or whither it goes (3.8). They do not know whence comes living water (4.11) or the water that was made wine (2.9). Above all, they do not know whence Jesus comes and whither he goes (4.14; 8.14; 9.29); even his disciples do not know whither he is going until he tells them (13.36; 14.5). It is he alone who knows (8.14; 13.3).

Certain Jerusalemites wrongly believe that they "know whence he is" and contrast him with the Messiah; no one knows whence the Messiah is. Jesus ironically tells them that they do know him, and know whence he is; but they do not know the one who sent him (7.25–28).

Gilles Wetter long ago argued that this "whence" and "whither" represent "a Gnostic formula in the Fourth Gospel," [39] but since most of the parallels he cites are from Stoic philosophers his proof is unconvincing.[40] Yet it remains true that the answer to the questions "whence" and "whither" in the gospel is quite unphilosophical. Jesus

knows "that he has come forth from God and that he is
returning to God" (13.3; see also 7.42). "I came forth from
the Father and came into the world; again I leave the world
and go to the Father" (16.28). His disciples reply, "We
believe that you came forth from God" (16.30).

A further answer to the question "whence" is given in
a passage where Jesus addresses his Jewish opponents. "You
are from below," he says (8.23); "I am from above; you are
from this world; I am not from this world." And the idea
is further developed in the "high-priestly" prayer in which
Jesus speaks of his disciples as given him by the Father
out of the world (17.6). "They are not from the world,
as I am not from the world" (17.16). Are these ideas Gnostic? They are very close to Gnostic ways of thinking, but
finally it is only Jesus whose origin is "from heaven." His
disciples, who in a Gnostic scheme would be Gnostics, are
indeed the recipients of revelation. But they are not recipients by nature. "I came as light into the world so that
everyone who believes in me might not remain in the darkness" (12.46; see also 8.12). "Walk while you have the
light, lest darkness overcome you; he who walks in darkness does not know whither he goes. While you have the
light, believe in the light, so that you may become sons of
light" (12.35–36). Man, like the darkness itself in the prologue, like the people of Israel, can choose whether to believe or not. There is a dualism here, but it is an ethical dualism. In spite of John's Gnostic language, he is a little closer
to Judaism than to Gnosticism.

The second significant point in John's semi-Gnostic language is his interpretation of the meaning of the cross. For Paul the cross is a stumbling-block, offensive to Jews and Greeks alike (1 Cor. 1.23). For John it is the way of Jesus' return to the Father. He uses the expression "to be lifted up" to signify at once the actual elevation of Jesus on the cross and his resurrection—ascension, which is one with his crucifixion. The cross is the way of life, a sign pointing to heaven. "As Moses raised up the serpent in the wilderness, so the Son of Man must be lifted up—so that by him everyone who believes may have eternal life" (3.14). The cross is like a magnet: "if I be lifted up from the earth, I will draw all men to myself" (12.32). And it is a means of giving knowledge: "when you lift up the Son of Man, then you will know that I AM" (8.28).

Does this mean that the cross is the gate of heaven, or rather that the ascended Jesus is the gate of heaven? He is "the way, the truth, and the life" (14.6) leading to his Father's house, in which there are many heavenly dwellings (14.2). He is also the gate in a parabolic allegory about sheep and a sheepfold, but we may doubt that there is any reference to heavenly gates or gate-keepers (10.7, 9).[41]

Even though the Gospel of John is not fully Gnostic, it remains a fact that in it we find a portrait of Jesus which is essentially mythological. If we ask ourselves what is really going on in this Gospel, apart from the demonstrations of divine power and the discourses which often explain the inner meaning of these demonstrations, apart from the oscillations between Galilee and Jerusalem, the answer is plain. It is a story of the descent of the redeemer from the invisible, unknown God above. He descends from heaven, and his appearance on earth as Jesus produces the judgment of the world and the defeat of Satan, the prince of this world. He returns above, exalted on the cross, to the heavenly house of his Father, and thereby opens the way to his disciples. In this form, the story is not one which any of the synoptic evangelists could have told. It is a story which lies close to what was told of Simon and of Menander. Yet it is a story which, though Gnostic and mythological in form, is not Gnostic in content. The dualism of this Gospel is always a limited dualism, recalling the Old Testament and some of the apocalyptic literature. The incarnate Word is a real man, who attends weddings and provides wine (2.1–11), is tired (4.6), weeps (11.35), is struck (18.22), and really dies (19.30, 34). How can such a gospel be classified?

Perhaps the solution lies in the relation of Judaism and Jewish Christianity to Gnosticism. The latter, we have argued, is a development out of the former, and we may not be too far wrong if we place John's Gospel somewhere between the two. Such a location will explain some of the passages which Bultmann treats as additions by an ecclesiastical redactor. Because John was not a thorough-going Gnostic, he could still write of the future resurrection and the last judgment. "Marvel not at this, for the hour comes when all those in the tombs will hear his voice and come out, those who have done good things to a resurrection of life, those who have done evil things to a resurrection of judgment" (5.28–29).[42] Because he was not a Gnostic, he could identify the "bread from heaven" with the flesh and blood of Jesus.[43] Because he was not a Gnostic, he could speak of water in connection with rebirth.[44]

The Gospel thus belongs to the history of Gnosticism only in the sense that it was used by Gnostics, who read into it speculations from a thought-world not altogether alien to that of the Evangelist himself. He himself, however, was no Gnostic.

JOHN AND PAUL

The difference between apocalyptic and Gnostic thought is most clearly evident in relation to God and the world. In both apocalypticism and Gnosticism there is considerable interest in cosmology, as we have seen. And it cannot be said that in Gnosticism there is no eschatology. The Apocryphon of John and the systems of Basilides and Valentinus provide clear evidence that Gnostics were deeply concerned with eschatological doctrines. But the crucial line of division lies in the discussion of God's control over the world. An apocalyptist can speak of Beliar or Satan as the god of this present evil *age*, but he awaits God's triumph over Beliar or Satan in this *world*. On the other hand, a Gnostic will speak of Satan as the god of this *world*. He will view the world, our earth, as permanently subject to the hostile angels, and will regard it as having been created by them. It is, so to speak, "by nature" evil, because it was created by evil powers. The temporal and ethical dualism of apocalyptic has become a physical and metaphysical dualism.

It is just here that the teaching of Paul and John can be differentiated. Paul speaks of Satan as "the god of this age" (2 Cor. 4.4) and mentions "the archons of this age" (1 Cor. 2.6–8). And while he once speaks of being "condemned with the world" (1 Cor. 11.32), and often uses the word "world" in an unfavorable sense, his thought remains just outside the domain of gnosis. He does not speak of the world's being necessarily hostile to God, its creator. On the other hand, John goes well beyond Paul. John never uses the word "aeon" except in phrases which mean "forever." And a strong dualism, at least an ethical dualism, occurs in his treatment of the cosmos. God made the cosmos, loved it, wanted to save it. But it was governed by an archon, Satan. In Paul's mind Satan was the archon of this *age;* but for John he has become the archon of this *world.* The unbelieving Jews, who are the children of the devil (8.44), are "of this world" (8.23). Only the disciples of Jesus, "begotten of God" (1.13), begotten from above by water and spirit (3.3–5), are not "of the world" (17.14–16). They can enter into the kingdom of God (3.5), which, like the kingdom of Jesus, is "not of this world" (18.36). This dualism, on the verge of becoming metaphysical, is even more strongly expressed in the First Epistle of John (2.16–17).

Everything in the world—the lust of the flesh and the lust of the eyes and the pride of life—is not of the Father but is of the world. And the world is passing away, as is its lust; but he who does the will of God remains forever.

In this passage we find an accent different from Paul's. Paul had said that the "constitution" (σχῆμα) of this world was passing away (1 Cor. 7.31), but he had meant that the hostile rulers of this age were being vanquished (2.6). John tells us that the world itself is passing away. Admittedly his eschatology remains ethical: "he who does the will of God remains forever." But he has come closer to Gnostic notions. "We know that we are of God, and the whole world lies in the evil one" (1 John 5.19)—even though "the victory which has conquered the world" is "our faith" (5.4).

The development from Paul's thought to John's is thus away from apocalyptic eschatology and in the direction of Gnosticism. Both remain un-Gnostic in so far as their dualism is temporal and ethical, in short, Jewish. Both come close to gnosis in so far as their dualism is on the verge of becoming both physical and metaphysical. John comes closer than Paul does.

IGNATIUS

The same process continues in the Christianity of the second century, notably in the writings of Ignatius of Antioch. It is significant that Ignatius seems to have known both the Pauline Epistles and the Gospel of John.[45] He also knows a good deal more. He tells the Trallians that he understands

"heavenly things and the angelic situations and the archontic associations and things visible as well as invisible" (5.2);
here his terminology has parallels both astrological and
gnostic. He informs the Smyrnaeans that there are archons
visible as well as invisible, and a "glory of the angels"; all
must believe in the blood of Christ unless they are to be
condemned (6.1).

The picture Ignatius provides of his opponents is fairly
obscure, but Einar Molland has shown that he is dealing
with one group, not with two.[46] These people are Judaizing
docetists, and at least some of them are gentiles.[47] They appeal to the Old Testament,[48] but apparently they treat it in
a haggadic manner [49] and provide non-Christian exegesis
of the prophets.[50] On the other hand, they say that Jesus
(or Christ?) merely seemed to suffer his crucifixion,[51] and
they do not admit that he "bore flesh." [52] They seem to
be concerned with "heavenly matters" such as "angelic lo-
cations" and "archontic conjunctions," which Ignatius also
calls "the glory of the angels" and "the archons visible and
invisible." [53] They abstain from the Eucharist because they
deny that it is the flesh of Jesus, which suffered for sins
and was raised by the Father.[54] Perhaps they even call themselves by the name of some Gnostic teacher.[55]

This teaching is hard to identify with any particular sect
we know. Criticism of those who say they are Jews but
are not is found in the Apocalypse of John (2.9; 3.9); such
men belong to "the synagogue of Satan." In 1 John 4.2 we
read of "spirits" which do not confess that Jesus Christ has
come in the flesh, and, like Ignatius, John criticizes loveless

schismatics who have separated from the community.[56] But it is not absolutely certain that we know the sect or sects attacked by John, though he may have in mind the Jewish Christian gnosis of Cerinthus. Ignatius may have something similar in view.

Of the archons, the "archon of this aeon" is given most attention by Ignatius. He is an archon who teaches a wicked doctrine (Eph. 17.1) and uses wicked arts and snares (Philad. 6.2) in his effort to tear Christians apart and to corrupt their minds away from God (Rom. 7.1). But he was ignorant of the virginity of Mary, of her giving birth, and of the death of the Lord, since these events took place in the Silence of God. By them magic was being destroyed, ignorance was being abolished, and the old kingdom was being destroyed; everything was being shaken (Eph. 19.1, 3).[57] The process of destruction continues on earth as in heaven. When Christians gather in worship, the powers of Satan are being destroyed and his destructive power is nullified by the harmony of faith. The peace characteristic of this worship brings to an end "every war of heavenly and earthly combatants" (Eph. 13.1–2).

It is difficult not to conclude that Ignatius knows, and partly accepts, a Gnostic interpretation of the meaning of the Incarnation. What he rejects is one basic Gnostic doctrine, the doctrine which John rejected, the doctrine that Christ merely seemed to suffer (Trall. 10.1; Smyrn. 2.1). In his discussions of the life of Jesus we can see what might be called haggadic notions springing up like weeds, notions of which Gnostics were also fond. For instance, "our God, Jesus the Christ," was baptized in order to purify the water (Eph. 18.2).[58] Again, "the Lord received ointment on his head so that he might breathe immortality on the church" (17.1). Jesus' head was anointed in Matthew 26.7; he breathed on the disciples in John 20.22. Ignatius combines the accounts and reads a Gnostic meaning into both.

We cannot call him exactly a Gnostic, but we cannot neglect the Gnostic elements in his thought, emphasized by Schlier[59] and well analyzed by Bartsch in his treatise on "Gnostic materials and church tradition in Ignatius."[60] Especially in relation to God and the heavenly regions and the archon of this aeon, not to mention the famous *obiter dictum* on the Eucharist as the "drug of immortality, the antidote for death" (Eph. 20.2), Ignatius seems to go beyond John in the direction of gnosis, a gnosis rather like that of Menander—in form but not in content.

Semi-Gnostic ideas occur even in relation to Ignatius' understanding of the episcopate. Henry Chadwick points out that "there is something almost comic in his insistence that when a bishop is saying nothing he is then to be regarded with special awe." But, as he adds, what Ignatius is doing is attributing the characteristics of God to the bishop; primeval silence is one of these; and in early Valentinianism the primal aeon Depth is accompanied by Silence.[61]

On the other hand, Ignatius' discussion of the star which shone more brightly than any other is not Gnostic in origin, though it may be Gnostic in intention. Following the lead of A. Cabaniss,[62] Père Daniélou has traced out the various

Jewish typological and prophetic notions which underlie the whole picture, fundamentally Jewish Christian.[63] One must agree that there is no "Gnostic myth" which underlies Ignatius' picture. But the whole passage (Eph. 19) lies on the borderline between Jewish apocalyptic and the Jewish Christian Gnosticism in which it later appears.[64]

7

BEYOND JUDAISM AND CHRISTIANITY: THE GOSPELS OF THOMAS, PHILIP, AND MARY

IN RECENT years we have been fortunate enough to acquire two "gospels" which make it possible to see the difference between the Christian interpretations of the meaning of Jesus and interpretations which definitely move in the direction of Gnosticism. These "gospels," included among the Nag-Hammadi documents, were first published photographically by Pahor Labib in 1956 but were not published in European languages until 1958 and 1959.[1] Meanwhile, considerable excitement had arisen about them, especially about the Gospel of Thomas. When scholars denied that it could be regarded as a "fifth Gospel," they inevitably gave the impression that it could be so viewed.

Actually, parts of the Greek text of this Gospel had long been known, though they had not been correctly identified; for the mysterious "sayings of Jesus," discovered among the Oxyrhynchus papyri at the beginning of this century, came from the Gospel of Thomas, as

H.-C. Puech was the first to point out.[2] Moreover, about twenty of the sayings in Thomas were also to be found in the writings of the Church Fathers, in semi-Christian apocryphal literature, and in Gnostic and Manichaean writings. Only with the discovery of the Gospel, however, could the various fragments be given a fairly precise location.

Is the Gospel of Thomas really a gospel? Certainly the scribe who copied the work in the fourth or fifth century so regarded it, for at the end he wrote the words, "Gospel of Thomas." It was probably known by this title in the third century, for Origen mentions—and rejects—a "Gospel according to Thomas."[3] But the book announces itself quite differently.

These are the secret words spoken by Jesus the Living;
and Didymus Judas Thomas wrote them down.
And he (Jesus) said,
"He who finds the interpretation of these words will not taste death."

The expression "the Living (One)" is used of Jesus in Revelation 1:17, where the risen Lord, as Son of Man, so describes himself to the disciple John. As often happens, a term apocalyptic in origin has been used by Gnostics for their own purposes—here as a semi-technical term for the risen Revealer. The "gospel" of Thomas, then, is a collection of sayings which constitute the secret revelation given by Jesus to his disciples after the resurrection. He speaks of himself as "the Living" again in Saying 59 (60): "Look upon the Living One as long as you live."[4] He will go away from them, according to Saying 12 (11), but meanwhile they enjoy his revelation which explains to them their true nature and destiny. Since the sayings are given in a post-resurrection setting, it was only natural for a Gnostic to refrain from including any materials which deal directly with the birth, life, and death of Jesus. But these materials are essential to the structure and the content of the canonical gospels. The basic question is whether "gospel" is to be defined in relation to the canonical writings or is to be given a "broader" meaning inclusive of such documents as this. In other words, if a "gospel" does not necessarily include reference to the earthly ministry of Jesus, this is a gospel.

Ordinarily, in early Christian literature the term "gospel" refers either to what Jesus himself proclaimed (Mark 1:14–15, etc.) or to the good news of his saving work. It is conceivable that the use of the term as a description of Thomas could be justified on the ground that it represents the message of Jesus. More striking is the unusual employment of the word in the Didache, or Teaching of the Apostles, from the late first century or the early second. Here the word refers to the "gospel" which contains the teaching of the Lord—implicitly about fasting (8.1), explicitly about prayer (8.2; 15.4), almsgiving (15.4), and dealing with recalcitrant brethren (15.3), as well as the reception of itinerant apostles and prophets (11.3).[5] We should not expect to find missionaries discussed in Thomas, but it may be significant that fasting, prayer, and almsgiving are treated, and all of them, as we shall see, are rejected. This difference marks a contrast between Jewish Christianity and Gnosis.

Many of the sayings in Thomas have parallels in the canonical gospels—especially in the synoptics, and among them especially in Luke. The question naturally arises:

do the sayings in Thomas come from the synoptic gospels
or from traditions independent of—perhaps even prior to
—these books? A striking feature of Thomas's parallels
is his tendency to combine sayings found separately in
our gospels and also to change the order of the sayings
found in any one book. Such combinations and alterations
were common among Christian writers of the second century, but they were especially characteristic of Gnostics.
An excellent example is provided by the Naassenes, who
also made use of Thomas.[6]

Unless you drink my blood and eat my flesh	John 6:53–56 (changed; flesh and blood reversed in order)
you will not enter into the kingdom of heaven;	Matt. 5:20, 18:3; John 3:5 as quoted by second-century writers
but if you drink the cup which I drink	Mark 10:38 (a question)
where I go, there you cannot enter.	John 8:21, 13:33

Examples like this (and they could be multiplied) show
at least the possibility that Thomas took gospel materials
and rearranged them for his own purposes.

Positive proof that he did so seems to be provided in
Saying 14.

If you go into every land, and travel in the regions,	(Matt. 10:11; Luke 10:1)
if they receive you,	
eat what is set before you.	Luke 10:8
Heal the sick among them,	Luke 10:8
for what goes into your mouth will not defile you,	Luke 10:9
but what goes out of your mouth, that will defile you.	Mark 7:15; Matt. 15:11

The statement about healing the sick has nothing to do with the context in Thomas; it is relevant only in Luke's collection of sayings. Therefore, Thomas copied it from Luke.

We are not concerned so much with the sources of the sayings in Thomas, however, as with their function in the extant work. What are the secrets which Jesus reveals in this gospel? And what bearing do they have on the theory of Gnostic origins which we have advocated? First of all, the Old Testament and its eschatology have been eliminated; Jesus is no Messiah but "like a righteous angel," "like a wise philosopher," or simply incomparable (Saying 13/12). Indeed, when the disciples state that "twenty-four prophets spoke in Israel, and all of them spoke concerning you," Jesus tells them that they "have forsaken the Living One and have spoken about the dead" (Saying 52/53). Gärtner has well identified the twenty-four as the authors of the canonical books of the Old Testament, contrasted with seventy secret books in the apocalypse of Ezra (2 Esdras [4 Ezra] 14:44–48).[7] Perhaps, as I have elsewhere suggested, they consist of twenty-three prophets and John the Baptist.[8] In any event, the Old Testament revelation is completely outmoded. What counts is the new revelation of the Gnostic Jesus.

Jews and Pharisees are alike rejected (Sayings 43/44, 39/40, 102/99); more than that, the Jewish practices of fasting, prayer, almsgiving, dietary observance and ritual washing are not to be followed (6/5, 14, 89, 104/101); circumcision is pointless (53/54). Fasting and Sabbath-observance have a purely "spiritual" meaning (27/28). Similarly, the temple has become so irrelevant that a saying about its destruction (71/72) now refers to the physical body or to the world.[9]

The Kingdom of God is no longer an eschatological reality. It has become a present, "spiritual" phenomenon. It is "spread out upon the earth and men do not see it" (113/111). It is not in the heaven or in the sea (3/2; cf. Rom. 10:6–7) but "within you and outside you." The inwardness of the Kingdom is derived, in Gnostic exegesis, from Luke 17:21; the outwardness probably refers to its heavenly or incomprehensible nature.[10] In any event, it is *not* future, but present.

> "On what day will the repose of the dead take place?
> and on what day will the new world (*kosmos*) come?"
> He said to them,
> "That for which you are waiting has come,
> but you do not recognize it" (Saying 51/52).

The new world was not simply inaugurated with the mission or the resurrection of Jesus; it has come and is fully present.

Entrance into it comes when the Gnostic, who has come from the Light above (50/51), knows himself (3/2) and does the will of the Father (99/96). The will of the Father includes becoming like a child (46/47)—and becoming like a child involves abolishing sexual distinctions.

When you make the two one,
and when you make the inside like the outside
and the outside like the inside,
and the upper like the lower,
and when you make the male and the female into a single one,
so that the male will not be male
and the female will not be female . . .
then you will enter the Kingdom (22/23).

When you undress yourselves and are not ashamed,
and take your clothing,
and lay it under your feet,
like little children,
and tread on it—
then you will be sons of the Living One
and you will have no fear (37/38).

Indeed, Jesus says of Mary (presumably Mary Magdalene, as in most Gnostic revelations) that he will make her a male so that she may become a "living spirit" like the male apostles: "for every woman who makes herself a man will enter into the Kingdom of Heaven" (114/112). According to the Naassenes, spiritual beings will come to "the house of God"; there they will cast off their garments and all of them will become bridegrooms, having been made male by the virginal Spirit.[11] This teaching is close to that of Thomas.

It need hardly be said that in Thomas as a whole there is hostility toward the world, toward the body, and toward man's physical existence in the world. Indeed, Jesus was apparently not "born of woman" (15)—or, at any rate, as revealer he had another mother than Mary (101/98).[12]

In Thomas, then, as among the Naassenes we are well beyond Judaism, as we have already suggested (p. 201, n. 31); we are also well beyond Christianity, for the secret revelation of the Living One has replaced the gospel story of the life, death, and resurrection of Jesus. Ascetic Gnostic sectarianism has replaced the life of the Church. Thomas contains a parable about a "wise fisherman" who threw away all the little fish he caught and kept only a large and good one (Saying 8/7); this may be contrasted with the parable of the Dragnet in Matthew 13:47–50, where good and bad fish are kept together until the end of the age. The Gnostic community is very small. It consists of those chosen by Jesus, "one out of a thousand and two out of ten thousand" (23/24)—a saying quoted by the Gnostic followers of Basilides and in *Pistis Sophia*.[13] To be sure, this element of exclusiveness is not absent from early Christianity ("many are called, but few are chosen"), but in Christianity it is balanced by the call to mission and discipleship, omitted in Thomas. The Gospel of Thomas thus offers no hope, eschatological or other, to mankind as a whole, or to any considerable numbers of men.

Since we have already suggested (Chapter 6) that the teaching of Jesus was not so thoroughly eschatological as some of our gospels make it, we may wonder whether Thomas does not represent a true interpretation of Jesus. Several factors militate against such a conclusion: (1) Thomas relies not on some early tradition of the sayings of Jesus but upon our gospels, which he "de-eschatologizes." (2) While Jesus' teaching may not have been completely centered upon the future, it did contain futuristic elements. His eschatology was not completely "realized" but, as we have said after Dodd, was "in process of realization." Matthew, for example, may exaggerate the future aspect of his teaching, but there was something there, as there was not in Thomas, to be exaggerated. At the same time, it must be recognized that Thomas too sometimes builds upon authentic aspects of the teaching of Jesus (obviously so, in the case of many doctrines taken over from the canonical gospels). He undoubtedly lays excessive emphasis upon the "inner" kingdom of God; but a certain emphasis upon such inwardness is already to be found in the Pauline epistles. To say that a Gnostic writing reflects some authentic Christian motifs, however, is not to say that the Gnostic synthesis is Christian. It develops only one side of the Christian tradition.[14]

The other "gospel" published by Labib is called "gospel of Philip."[15] This book has even less to do with Philip than Thomas has to do with Thomas. Philip is mentioned only once, and nothing is made of him as a transmitter of revelation—though in *Pistis Sophia* (42–44) he has a role of this kind. This "gospel" does not contain the one fragment of a "gospel of Philip" which we possess, one found in the *Panarion* of Epiphanius.[16] Instead, in an order which may be intentionally confused, we find bits of Gnostic myth, sayings ascribed to Jesus, Gnostic exegesis of New Testament passages, and discussions of the sacred rites of baptism, unction, eucharist, and spiritual marriage.[17]

As H.-M. Schenke has pointed out, this gospel is essentially Valentinian, though eclectic; it contains materials from other systems. Some of its most interesting features find few parallels in Valentinian documents. Chief among these, perhaps, is the series of statements about the relation of the Gnostic to Judaism and Christianity. The Gnostic is strongly conscious of his non-gentile nature. "A gentile does not die, for he has never lived. . . . He who has come to believe in the truth has found life, and he runs the risk of dying because he lives" (4). At the same time, the Gnostic is beyond Judaism. "He who has not received the Lord is still a Hebrew" (46). "When we were Hebrews, we were orphans (cf. John 14:18). But when we became Christians, we acquired Father and Mother" (cf. Mark 10:30).[18] To become a Christian, i.e., a Gnostic Christian, means leaving both the gentile world and Judaism behind.

If you say, "I am a Jew" (cf. Acts 22:3), no one will be moved. If you say, "I am a Roman" (cf. Acts 22:25–29), no one will be troubled. If you say, "I am a Greek, a barbarian, a slave, a freeman" (cf. Col. 3:11), no one will be agitated. If you say, "I am a Christian," he will tremble . . . (49).

But ordinary Christian terms do not mean what ordinary Christians suppose. "Christ," for example, is the Greek equivalent of the Syriac "Messiah," which is taken to mean "the measured one." "Jesus" in Hebrew means "salvation" (cf. Matt. 1:21). And "the Nazorean" or "the Nazarene" is understood as meaning "the one who belongs to the truth" or "the one revealed in concealment" (47 and 19). Indeed, one must recognize that even the Valentinian name for Sophia, "Achamoth," must be used with care. Achamoth is the real Sophia above, but there is also a lower Sophia, the Sophia of Death—for "mōth" in Hebrew means "death" (39).

The names which men ordinarly give even to Father, Son, Holy Spirit, Life, Light, Resurrection, and Church involve error, for they are understood in relation to transitory manifestations, not eternal realities (11). Men do not understand that Christ contained (and secretly conveyed) hidden meanings for all things; he "has everything in himself (cf. Col. 1:16–17): man, angel, mystery, and the Father" (cf. John 14:10). Similarly, "the Lord brought everything in a mystery: baptism, unction, eucharist, redemption, bride-chamber" (20 and 68). This element of mystery meant that he revealed himself not as he was but as men could see him (26).[19] It also meant that ordinary Christian ideas about him are often wrong, for example in regard to his origin, his life, and his end.

Those who say that Mary became pregnant of the Holy Spirit are wrong because no female being (Mary) ever became pregnant from another female (the Holy Spirit).[20] The Lord actually had two fathers, one of them his "Father in heaven" (17; contradicted on 83). During his ministry he was always accompanied by three Mary's: his mother, his sister, and the Magdalene; the last of them was his "consort," whom he often kissed; she became spiritually pregnant and perfect (pp. 31, 32, 55). He loved her more than the disciples. Finally, some say that the Lord first died and then rose. This view is wrong, for if anyone does not attain to the resurrection (cf. Phil. 3:11) he will die. Indeed, if anyone does not first receive resurrection, while he is still alive, he will receive nothing at death (pp. 21 and 90). Evidently this last notion is based on the Johannine doctrine of resurrection (John 11:24–26).

The passages we have cited indicate that, at least in large measure, the teaching of the "gospel of Philip" is a conscious reinterpretation of the teaching of the early Christian church, in the light of deeper meanings to be found in Gnostic systems. From the materials in Philip alone we cannot tell whether the Gnosticism preceded or followed the Christianity, though it would seem likely that it was developed later.

What of the strange remarks about Hebrews? These may be compared with the statement ascribed to Basilidians by Irenaeus.[21] "They say that they are no longer Jews but are not yet Christians." Should this remark be taken literally or symbolically, or both? Certainly these Gnostics, or their predecessors, knew something about the Old Testament. They believed that "the prophecies were spoken by the world-making principalities, and the law by their chief, the one who led the people out of the land of Egypt." They knew that the Hebrew text of Isaiah 28:10 contains lexicographical mysteries, for they used one of the obscure words in it as "the name in which the Saviour descended and ascended." More than that, they seem to have used something like Psalm 2 (see 62 and 105) for a frame to their picture of Jesus. "The God of the Jews" wanted to subjugate the other nations to his people; therefore the rest of the principalities stood up and resisted him. Is not this related to Psalm 2:2, "the kings of the earth rose up and the archons took counsel together against the Lord?" When Simon of Cyrene was crucified in the place of Jesus, Jesus as Simon stood by and laughed at the crucifiers, as in Psalm 2:4 "he who sits in the heavens laughs," and "the Lord has them in derision." So Jesus derided those who wanted to hold him, for he could not be held. "Let us break their bonds asunder and cast their cords from us" (Ps. 2:3). This is to say that these Gnostics, like Saturninus, made use of the Jewish scriptures in order to develop their system.

We cannot be certain that the Basilidians were actually ex-Jews, but it is fairly clear that their concern for the Old Testament—in part, the Hebrew Old Testament—is

neither Christian nor pagan. Would someone who was not
an ex-Jew have said that he was? And *if* these Basilidians
can be regarded as ex-Jews, we can probably proceed to
claim that some elements, at least, which have gone into
the "gospel of Philip" have come from ex-Hebrews. We
cannot lay much emphasis upon remarks about the temple
in Jerusalem, with its "holy" and its "holy of holies" (e.g.,
on 76), for statements about the Holy of Holies seem to
be based upon the Epistle to the Hebrews and others,
about the veil, on the gospel accounts. The pictures of
Adam's origin, of life and the trees in paradise, of the
separation of Eve from Adam, of her seduction by the
serpent—all these owe something to Jewish and, specifically, Gnostic exegesis of Genesis; but once more there
are clearly Christian elements in the narratives. Christ
was born of a virgin because Adam originated from two
virgins, the Spirit and "virgin earth" (83). The tree of
knowledge was the law; instead of giving Adam the knowledge of good and evil, it simply prepared death for those
who ate from it (94). This looks like a Gnostic interpretation of the seventh chapter of Romans. There was food
for the animals in paradise, but no food for men until
Christ, the Perfect Man, brought bread from heaven (15;
based on John 6). Finally, the notion that Eve's separation from Adam marked the beginning of death is clearly
based on a contrast between the original creation of the
man in God's image and the secondary creation of Eve
from Adam; but the speculation has been influenced by
the gospel prohibition of divorce. Christ came to rectify
the separation which arose "from the beginning" (78; cf.
Mark 10:6; Matt. 19:4). "Those who have united them-

selves in the bridechamber cannot be separated again"
(79, οὐκέτι; Mark 10:8–9; Matt. 19:6).

Some of the atmosphere of Philip, then, is Jewish; but
it is more evidently Christian in derivation. Indeed, it may
be added that the emphasis upon the holy kiss is Christian,
not Jewish at all.[22] But this is what we should expect to
find in a late Gnostic document. The wonder is not that
there are so few purely Jewish elements, but that there
are any references at all to Hebrews or Jews.

Another Gnostic gospel recently published deserves
mention: this is the Gospel of Mary, almost certainly Mary
Magdalene. Once more we have a Coptic text (incom-
plete) and a Greek fragment of the third century.[23] The
Saviour tells Mary that matter will be destroyed and explains to Peter that sin as such is non-existent. In this
context we encounter words of the Saviour which express
the Gnostic transformation of eschatology.[24]

Peace be with you (John 20:21). Receive my peace for yourselves. Take heed lest anyone lead you astray with the words,
"Lo, here!" or "Lo, there!" (cf. Luke 17:21), for the Son of
Man is within you (cf. Luke 17:21). Follow him; those who
seek him will find him (cf. Matt. 7:7). Go, therefore, and
proclaim the gospel of the Kingdom (cf. Mark 16:15). I have
left no commandment but what I have commanded you (cf.
John 13:34), and I have left no law, as the lawgiver did,
lest you be bound by it.

Only Mary Magdalene accepts this "gospel" which has
made men of her and the other disciples.[25] She ought to
understand it, for the Saviour loved her more than other
women, indeed more than the other disciples.[26]

The "gospel," then, is properly Mary's. It is a gospel

in which apocalyptic eschatology is replaced by Gnostic inwardness and, at the same time, freedom from law. The kingdom of God within (Luke) is even replaced by the inner Son of Man who resembles the inner man or the inner Christ of the apostle Paul—or the Christ of the Naassenes, "in all created things imprinted as Son of Man from the Unimprinted One." [27]

In all three of these gospels is reflected the strenuous Gnostic effort to remove apocalyptic elements from the Christian gospel and to treat eschatology as already realised.

CONCLUSION

OF ALL the Fathers of the second century, Ignatius probably came closest to Gnostic ways of thinking. When we see what seem to resemble Gnostic ideas in the works of later writers, we should bear in mind van Unnik's wise warning that a phrase used by a Gnostic teacher is not necessarily a Gnostic phrase.[1] There are many ordinary Christian theologoumena in the writings of the Valentinians, for example. By the same token, phrases used by more orthodox writers are not necessarily Christian. Indeed, the development of Christian theology in the second century was a process which owed a great deal to Gnostic teachers. Harnack claimed that they were the first Christian theologians,[2] and he was right, at least in the sense that they posed some of the problems which others solved in a different way.

Among the modern scholars who have laid special emphasis on the close relations between Gnostic and Christian theologians of the second century and the third, we need mention only the names of A. Houssiau, G. Kretschmar, J. Daniélou, and A. Orbe. Houssiau has shown that Irenaeus owed to the Christological thought of the Valentinian Ptolemaeus; Kretschmar has pointed to the Gnostic origins

of some early Christian thinking about the Trinity; Daniélou has indicated that a good deal of Jewish-Christian
theology was shared by orthodox writers with the Gnostics; and Orbe has traced the doctrine of the procession of
the Word through Gnostic and orthodox writers alike,
reaching the paradoxical conclusion that sometimes the
Gnostics expressed the orthodox doctrine, or certain aspects
of it, more satisfactorily than did their orthodox contem-
poraries. The great Gnostic errors lay in their conceptions
of man rather than in their speculations about the divine
nature.[3]

It is also important to notice the breadth of what H. E. W.
Turner has called the penumbra between orthodoxy
and heresy.[4] Apocryphal gospels and acts provide obvious
examples; so does the Ascension of Isaiah; so does the
Epistle of the Apostles. More than that, while the apologist
Justin militantly attacked Simonians and Marcionites, there
are many passages in his writings which a Valentinian
would have found attractive. Justin's pupil Tatian became
a Gnostic after his master's death. And in the writings of
Clement and Origen it is easy enough to find traces of
indebtedness to the Valentinians. To be sure, Justin, Tatian,
Clement, and Origen were not Valentinians. None of
them, except possibly Tatian, was in any way enthusiastic
about Valentinianism. But this kind of gnosis was in the
air they breathed, and some of it entered their lungs.

For the most part, it was not theologians but the Church
itself which acted against Gnosticism. The Church gradually developed authoritative lists of acceptable books and
authoritative credal formulas as norms for interpreting
scripture, and relied on an apostolic ministry to do the
interpreting. All these weapons had to be developed, if not

created, by the Church in its struggle against Gnostic teaching.

And it was in the course of this struggle that, under the leadership of the Roman church, Christian orthodoxy was formulated and was victorious. The triumph of orthodoxy meant the triumph of the created world over the aeons,[5] of collective experience over individual freedom, of history over the freely creative imagination, of objectivity over subjectivity. Something was lost. The creative freedom of the religious imagination was more completely channeled in the service of an institution, and anyone who turns from the New Testament, especially the writings of Paul and John, to most patristic literature immediately encounters a certain flatness and lack of life. Similarly, one can contrast Ignatius with his more "orthodox" contemporary Clement of Rome. This change is not due to "Hellenization" alone; it is due to the necessity for conformity, without which the Church could not have survived, but with which the Church has sometimes been more concerned with self-preservation than with proclaiming the newness of a new creation. The freshness of grace has been subordinated to the claims of nature. Yet something was certainly gained. The rule of God over history and nature could be asserted by the Church as by no Gnostic group. The goodness, actual and potential, of the creation and of human existence could be affirmed. The reality and meaningfulness of historical events could be proclaimed. In other words, orthodox Christians could hold, as Gnostics could not, that this world is neither heaven nor hell.

Gnosticism did not provide an adequate answer to the problems of human existence. Aside from its fanciful mythology, its notion that the Gnostic is essentially and indeed entirely a spiritual being does not correspond with what was known of human nature even in antiquity. Its emphasis upon salvation as escape meant that human life was treated neither deeply nor broadly enough.

Sometimes, to be sure, the Church Fathers who reacted against Gnosticism went too far in their insistence upon the imminent approach of God's reign over the created world. Thus, Irenaeus was favorably disposed toward Montanism and Tertullian became a Montanist; and Montanism was a revival of apocalyptic enthusiasm in the latter half of the second century.[6] But it can hardly be affirmed that this tendency was more dangerous than its opposite, a theology or group of theologies which denied the unity of God, his creative power, his love, his work of redemption, and the potential goodness of the created world and of life in it.

The significance of the rejection of gnosis by church and synagogue alike lies partly in the Western and Hebrew-Christian recognition of the reality of time and space, but most of all, I believe, in the continuing worship of God the Father Almighty, Maker of heaven and earth. Against all Gnostic attacks the Church retained the Old Testament and insisted that the story of Jesus could not be understood in purely symbolical terms. The Church was itself catholic, that is to say, universal; it did not view itself as a coterie of the spiritually élite. There was, of course, a place for the individual within the community; of Jesus, Paul says, "He loved me and gave himself for me" (Gal. 2.20). But the last word is expressed by the evangelist who comes close to gnosis but rejects it: "God so loved the world that he gave his only Son, so that all who believe in him might not perish but have everlasting life" (John 3.16).

NOTES

The following abbreviations are used in Notes and in the Bibliography:

HTR   Harvard Theological Review
JTS   Journal of Theological Studies
RE   Real-Encyclopädie der classischen Altertumswissenschaft
VC   Vigiliae Christianae
ZNW   Zeitschrift für die Neutestamentliche Wissenschaft

Notes to Chapter 1: THE NATURE OF GNOSTICISM

1. See, for example, K. Stendahl, ed., *The Scrolls and the New Testament* (New York, 1957); F. M. Cross, *The Ancient Library of Qumran* (New York, 1958).

2. Justin *Apologies* and *Dialogue;* Irenaeus *Adversus haereses;* Hippolytus *Refutatio;* Epiphanius *Panarion;* Theodore bar Konai, in H. Pognon, tr., *Inscriptions mandaïtes des coupes de Khouabir* (Paris, 1898), pp. 159–232. The following are also valuable: Völker, *Quellen zur Geschichte der christlichen Gnosis;* Sagnard, *La gnose valentinienne et le témoignage de saint Irénée* and *Clément d'Alexandrie: Extraits de Théodote;* Quispel, ed. and tr., *Ptolémée: Lettre à Flora.* The account of Gnostic systems in Irenaeus *Adv. haer.* 1.23–31 deserves to be edited with a commentary.

3. *The Gnostics and Their Remains* (2d ed.; London, 1887), p. 409.

4. *Pistis Sophia.*

5. *Philotesia Paul Kleinert* (Berlin, 1907), pp. 315–36.

6. *Die gnostischen Schriften des koptischen Papyrus Berolinensis 8502.*

7. F. L. Cross, ed. and tr., *The Jung Codex.*

8. *Gospel of Truth.*

9. Labib, *Coptic Gnostic Papyri in the Coptic Museum at Old Cairo,* Vol. I.

10. "Les nouveaux écrits gnostiques découverts en Haute-Egypte," *Coptic Studies in Honour of Walter Ewing Crum,* pp. 91–154.

11. *Les livres secrets des gnostiques d'Egypte.*

12. See also C. Bonner, "Magical Amulets," HTR, XXXIX (1946), 25–53.

13. M. Summers, *A History of Witchcraft* (New York, 1956), pp. 28–29.

14. *Strom.* VII.108.1–2; see also Justin *Dial.* 35.6. But according to Origen (*Commentary on Matthew* XI.5), "Peratikoi" is a mystical interpretation of "Hebrews."

15. Irenaeus *Adv. haer.* 1.21.4 (Harvey p. 186); Clement *Excerpta ex Theodoto* 78.2; for Johannine parallels see Chapter 6.

16. Greek philosophy and religion might hold that the soul was in a body because of previous sin (see, for example, E. Norden, *Aeneis Buch VI* [Leipzig, 1916], pp. 18–20); the Gnostic point was that the sin was someone else's.

17. Hippolytus *Ref.* VIII.15.1–2 (italics mine).

18. *Ibid.,* V.26.35.

19. Kerényi, *Mythologie und Gnosis* (*Albae Vigiliae,* Vol. XIV [Amsterdam, 1942]), p. 42; Irenaeus *Adv. haer.* 1.11.1, 18.1, 21.5 (Harvey pp. 98, 169, 188).

20. Jonas, *Gnosis und spätantiker Geist,* Vols. I and II.

21. Gospel of Truth, p. 22.3–19.

22. Puech, "The Jung Codex and the Other Gnostic Documents from Nag Hammadi," in Cross, ed. and tr., *The Jung Codex,* p. 33.

23. See also Schoeps, *Urgemeinde—Judenchristentum—Gnosis,* pp. 30–35; Nilsson, *Geschichte der griechischen Religion,* II, 586–89.

24. Eusebius *Ecclesiastical History* iv.22.4, 7.

25. Thomas, *Le mouvement baptiste en Palestine et Syrie,* pp. 40–42.

26. *Dial.* 80.4.

27. "Sur deux hérésies juives mentionnés par Justin Martyr," *Revue d'Histoire et de Philosophie Religieuses,* XVIII (1938), 54–58.

28. "Les sectes juives d'après les témoignages patristiques," *Texte und Untersuchungen,* LXIII (1957), 526–39.

29. Without raising the question of the influence of expression on what is being expressed.

30. *Adv. haer.* 1.23–24 (Harvey pp. 190–98).

31. On the word, see Kittel, *Theologisches Wörterbuch zum Neuen Testament,* I, 81; G. F. Moore, Judaism (Cambridge, Mass., 1927), I, 381. On man, see H. A. Wolfson, *Philo* (Cambridge, Mass., 1947), I, 187; Justin *Dial.* 62.3. See also Quispel, "Der gnostische Anthropos und die jüdische Tradition," *Eranos Jahrbücher,* XXII (1954), 204–5.

32. See, for example, Jubilees 1.27; Gal. 3.19; Acts 7.53; Heb. 2.2. But not Josephus (see W. D. Davies, "A Note on Josephus, Antiquities 15:136," HTR, XLVII [1954], 135–40; F. R. Walton, "The Messenger of God in Hecataeus of Abdera," HTR, XLVIII [1955], 255–57).

33. See, for example, Ezek. 40.3; Zech. 1.9; Dan. 9.22.

34. *Théologie du Judéo-Christianisme.*

35. Clement *Strom.* v.77.2.

36. Origen *Commentary on John* ii.31; an apocalyptic-

eschatological fragment in Eusebius *Praeparatio Evangelica*
VI.11.64: "I read on the tablets of heaven what will happen to
you and your sons." The fragments are not Archontic, against
A. Resch, *Agrapha* (Leipzig, 1906), pp. 296–97.

37. Hippolytus *Ref.* v.26–27; Haenchen, "Das Buch Baruch," *Zeitschrift für Theologie und Kirche*, L (1953), 123–58;
R. M. Grant, "Gnosis Revisited," *Church History*, XXIII
(1954), 36–45.

38. Hippolytus *Ref.* v.26.2.

39. J. Bonsirven, *Exégèse rabbinique et exégèse paulinienne*
(Paris, 1939), pp. 214–25.

40. *Ibid.*, pp. 218–19 (*Canticles Rabbah*).

41. Hippolytus *Ref.* v.27.4; see also v.26.36–37.

42. We know no system without Jesus, however.

43. Williams, "Eznik's Résumé of Marcionite Doctrine,"
JTS, XLV (1944), 65–73.

44. Similarly many Gnostics regarded themselves as Christians, or the only true Christians, but were not so regarded by
authorized teachers.

45. Josephus *Bell.* II.118; see also *Ant.* XVIII.23.

46. Philo *Leg. ad Gaium* 337.

47. Josephus *Ant.* xx.97–98. Christian prophets were content
to predict the famine (Acts 11.27–30).

48. Josephus *Bell.* II.261–63; *Ant.* xx.169–72.

49. Josephus *Bell.* VI.290–306.

50. *Ibid.*, IV.154.

51. *Ibid.*, II.567; III.11.

52. *Ibid.*, II.152–53.

53. *Ibid.*, VI.289.

54. *Ibid.*, XI.6–7.

55. *Ibid.*, VI.285–86.

56. *Ibid.*, VII.409–11.

57. *Ibid.*, VII.437–50.

58. Dio Cassius *Hist.* LXIII.5.2; F. Cumont, "L'iniziazione di

Nero da parte di Tiridate d'Armenia," *Rivista di filologia*, LXI (1933), 145–54.

59. Tacitus *Hist.* v.13; Suetonius *Vesp.* iv.5; on Hystaspes, see J. Bidez and F. Cumont, *Les mages hellénisés* (Paris, 1938), I, 215–22; II, 359–76.

60. Tacitus *Hist.* ii.8; Suetonius *Nero* lvii:2; Dio Chrysostom *Or.* xxi.10.

61. *Bell.* iii.400–2; see also iii.351–52; vi.312–13.

62. Tacitus *Hist.* iv.54.

63. Hippolytus *Ref.* ix.13–16.

64. Groag, "Lusius (Quietus)," in RE, XIII, 1883–84.

65. For his name, see J. Milik, "Une lettre de Siméon bar Kokheba," *Revue Biblique*, LX (1953), 276–94.

66. Dio Cassius *Hist.* lxix.14.1.

67. For later periods, see M. Buttenwieser, "Apocalyptic Literature, Neo-Hebraic," in *Jewish Encyclopedia*, I, 675–85; S. W. Baron, *Social and Religious History of the Jews*, II, 89–171; V, 138–208.

68. A. Reifenberg, *Ancient Jewish Coins* (Jerusalem, 1947), pp. 28–38, 57–66.

69. See also H. St. J. Hart, "Judaea and Rome: The Official Commentary," JTS, N.S. III (1952), 172–98.

70. *The Old Rabbinic Doctrine of God* (London, 1927), I, 171–72.

71. "Prophecy, Apocalyptic, and the Historical Hour," *Union Seminary Quarterly Review*, XII, No. 3 (March, 1957), 16–18.

72. Josephus *Bell.* vii.376.

73. S. Slotkin, *The Peyote Religion* (Glencoe, Ill., 1956), pp. 1–7, 15.

74. L. Festinger *et al.*, *When Prophecy Fails* (Minneapolis, 1956), especially p. 221.

75. R. M. Grant, *The Letter and the Spirit* (London, 1957), pp. 18–30.

76. Hippolytus *Ref.* v.6–8; vi.19.2–3.
77. Daniélou, *Théologie du Judéo-Christianisme*, p. 86.

Notes to Chapter 2: THE HEAVENLY WORLD

1. See also W. H. Brownlee, *The Dead Sea Manual of Discipline* (New Haven, 1951), pp. 38–41.
2. M. Burrows, *The Dead Sea Scrolls* (New York, 1955), p. 239.
3. See also F. Boll, "Hebdomas," RE, VII, 2547–78.
4. Origen *Contra Celsum* v.52.54.
5. *Pistis Sophia* 99, 134.
6. See also Söderberg, *La religion des Cathares*, pp. 130 n.1, 131.
7. D. Flusser, "The Apocryphal Book of Ascensio Isaiae and the Dead Sea Sect," *Israel Exploration Journal*, III (1953), 30–47.
8. Epiphanius *Pan.* xl.2.2.
9. Note that Irenaeus *Adv. haer.* ii.24.2 (Harvey p. 336) regards Baruch as the name of God.
10. Apocryphon of John, pp. 33–34; Irenaeus *Adv. haer.* i.29.2 (Harvey p. 223); Raguel in Enoch 20.
11. Enoch 82.13–20 (Oriares in Enoch 78.1). F. C. Grant compares the Zealot slogan with Milkiel and Elimelech; for the antiquity of the former, see O. Eissfeldt, "Malkiel (König ist El) und Malkija," *Atti del' VIII Congresso Internazionale di Storia delle Religioni*, pp. 261–63.
12. See also L. Ginzberg, *The Legends of the Jews* (Philadelphia, 1939), VI, 82 n.440.
13. Doresse, "Trois livres gnostiques inédits," VC, II (1948), 141–42.
14. C. Bonner, *Studies in Graeco-Roman Magical Amulets* (Ann Arbor, 1950), p. 325.
15. ΕΙΣ ΘΕΟΣ (Göttingen, 1926), pp. 241–53.
16. The conjecture goes back to Bursian; the only manu-

script reads: "abrax aslo therbeeo" (Hyginus *Fab.* 183). See also Macrobius *Sat.* 1.18.18–21.

17. Origen *Contra Celsum* VI.30.

18. In Enoch 20, it is stated that Uriel, one of the seven, watches over the cosmos and Tartarus. For angels ταρταροῦχοι, see Hippolytus *Ref.* x.34.2 and M. R. James, "A New Text of the Apocalypse of Peter," JTS, XII (1910–11), 370.

19. Gen. 1.2; Isa. 34.11; Jer. 4.23.

20. Origen *Contra Celsum* VI.31.

21. Orac. Sib. 1.304, 316 (see also Beer, "Sabaoth," in RE, I A, 1535); Origen *Commentary on John* 1.31.

22. Bonner, *Studies in Graeco-Roman Magical Amulets*, pp. 136–38 and Fig. 188.

23. Plutarch *De Iside* 47; Bidez and Cumont, *Les mages hellénisés*, p. 71.

24. Zaehner, *Zurvan* (Oxford, 1955), pp. 158, 369, 400, 401, 404.

25. Apocryphon of John, p. 42.8; Irenaeus *Adv. haer.* 1.30.4 (Harvey p. 230).

26. Plutarch *De Iside* 46.

27. Apocryphon of John p. 40.2.

28. *Textes et monuments figurés relatifs aux mystères de Mithra* (Brussels, 1899), I, 74–85.

29. *Hauptprobleme der Gnosis*, pp. 351–55.

30. R. Pettazzoni, *Essays on the History of Religions* (Leyden, 1954), p. 183.

31. "Ahriman et le dieu suprême dans les mystères de Mithra," *Numen*, II (1955), 191.

32. "The Lion-Headed God of the Mithraic Mysteries," *Proc. Soc. Bibl. Arch.*, XXXIV (1912), 125–42.

33. *Ormazd et Ahriman* (Paris, 1953), pp. 126–29; see also "Ahriman et le dieu suprême dans les mystères de Mithra," *Numen*, II (1955), 190–95.

34. Zaehner, *Zurvan*, pp. viii–ix.

35. "Some Reflections on Zurvanism," *Bull. School of Oriental and African Studies,* XIX (1957), 314–16.

36. Origen *Contra Celsum* vi.22; Chadwick, tr., *Origen: Contra Celsum,* p. 335 n.2.

37. Pliny *Nat. hist.* xxviii.92; Bidez and Cumont, *Les mages hellénisés,* II, 196.

38. G. Dalman, *Aramäisch-neuhebräisches Handwörterbuch* (Frankfurt, 1922), 7b; for ass, 311a; fire, 45a; hyena, 357b (cf. 35a).

39. Apocryphon of John, p. 42.8.

40. Irenaeus *Adv. haer.* 1.16.1 (Harvey pp. 157–58).

41. *Hauptprobleme der Gnosis,* p. 341; Bidez and Cumont, *Les mages hellénisés,* II, 100.

42. Irenaeus *Adv. haer.* 1.17.1 (Harvey p. 166).

43. Enoch 78.15–16; Jubilees 6.30–32.

44. Irenaeus *Adv. haer.* 1.18.1 (Harvey pp. 169–70).

45. Jubilees 2.15, 23; see also Origen *Num. hom.* iv.1.

46. Enoch 78.15–16. Compare the place of Helen as the thirtieth disciple of John the Baptist (*Clem. hom.* II 2; J. Daniélou, "Les douze Apôtres et le zodiaque, " VC, XIII, 1959; 14–22).

47. Enoch 80.2–8.

48. Irenaeus *Adv. haer.* 1.17.1 (Harvey p. 166); see also F. Boll, *Sphaera* (Leipzig, 1903), p. 316 n.2; W. Gundel and H. Gundel, "Planeten," in RE, XX, 2091; *Genesis Rabbah* x.4.

49. *Adv. haer.* ii.24.4 (Harvey pp. 340–41).

50. For the latitude of Lyons, see Harvey in Irenaeus *Adv. haer.,* p. 341 n.2.

51. See, for example, *War of the Sons of Light against the Sons of Darkness,* p. 1.1.

52. *Manual of Discipline,* p. 1.23–24; see also *Zadokite Document,* p. 4.12–15.

53. Matt. 4.8–9; Luke 4.5–6.

54. See Bultmann, *Das Evangelium des Johannes,* pp. 240–44.

55. See the exegesis of Eulogius in Photius *Bibl.* 230 (*Patrologia Graeca* 103, 1073B-D).

56. Mastema is Beliar; see also *Zadokite Document*, p. 5.17–19: "Moses and Aaron continued in their charge, through the help of the Angel of Lights, even though Belial in his cunning had set up Jannes and his brother in opposition to them." On the name Mastema, see C. C. Torrey, *The Apocryphal Literature* (New Haven, 1945), pp. 127–29.

57. So Peter argues against Simon in *Clementine Recognitions* II.55. On the unity of God and the one temple, see Philo *Spec. Leg.* 1.67–68; Josephus *Contra Apionem* 1.193; on the one law and the one people, 2 Baruch 48.24; Justin *Dial.* 123.1 (S. Hanson, *The Unity of the Church in the New Testament* [Uppsala, 1946], pp. 12–14).

58. Apocryphon of John, pp. 38.14; 41.6–7; 42.10–11.

59. Irenaeus *Adv. haer.* 1.31.1 (Harvey p. 241).

60. This problem was raised in Jewish apocalyptic; see 2 Esdras 7.106–11

61. See also F. Cumont, *Lux Perpetua* (Paris, 1949).

62. Bousset, "Die Himmelsreise der Seele," *Archiv für Religionswissenschaft*, IV (1901), 136–69, 229–73.

63. In 2 Esdras 7.88–99, discarnate spirits have rest in seven "orders"; in the seventh, "greater than all that have been mentioned," they see God's face. See Daniélou, *Théologie du Judéo-Christianisme* (Paris, 1958), pp. 273–90.

64. *Ant.* 18.18.

65. *Spec. leg.* 1.13, cited by W. Gundel and H. Gundel, "Planeten," in RE, XX, 2121.

66. *Dial.* 36.5–6.

67. Epistle of the Apostles 13; Ascension of Isaiah 10.11; Irenaeus *Epideixis* 84.

68. Irenaeus *Adv. Haer.* 1.23.3, 30.12 (Harvey pp. 193, 238).

69. *Ibid.*, 1.21.5 (Harvey pp. 187–88); Origen *Contra Celsum* VI.31, with the commentary of Chadwick, *Origen: Contra Celsum*, pp. 346–48.

70. The Marcosian expression, "I am a precious vessel," is not necessarily Mandaean, for the Mandaeans were influenced by earlier Gnostic systems.

71. *Chagigah* 14b; *Canticles Rabbah* I.4.1.

72. Gospel of Truth, p. 43.1.

73. *Ibid.*, p. 43.10–11. See also the "Gnostic" goal in Clement *Strom.* VII.13.1, 57.5 (Stählin compares *Excerpta ex Theodoto* 63.1—a passage which is Valentinian).

74. Cf. the prayer of Joseph cited on p. 18.

75. Odeberg, *The Fourth Gospel*, pp. 89–90.

76. *Jesus and His Coming* (New York, 1957), p. 22; see also E. M. Sidebottom, "The Ascent and Descent of the Son of Man in the Gospel of St. John," *Anglican Theological Review*, XXXIX (1957), 115–22.

Notes to Chapter 3: SIMON MAGUS AND HELEN, HIS THOUGHT

1. See, for example, O. Cullmann, *Le problème littéraire et historique du roman pseudo-clémentin* (Paris, 1930), especially pp. 166–68.

2. I owe this reference to Professor Roy Bruenig.

3. *Adv. haer.* 1.23.1 (Harvey p. 191).

4. Acts. 8.4–25.

5. See also H. Conzelmann, *Die Mitte der Zeit* (Tübingen, 1954).

6. See also W. Bauer, *A Greek-English Lexicon of the New Testament and Other Early Christian Literature*, p. 207.

7. Peterson, ΕΙΣ ΘΕΟΣ, pp. 268–70.

8. Josephus *Ant.* XVIII.85–87.

9. *Apol.* 1.26.56.

10. H. Dessau, *Inscriptiones Latinae Selectae*, II, Part 1 (Berlin, 1902), 3474.

11. S. B. Platner and T. Ashby, *A Topographical Dictionary of Ancient Rome* (Oxford, 1929), p. 469.

12. Another point is that the god was sometimes called "Sanctus" as well as "Sancus" (Dessau, *Inscriptiones Latinae Selectae*, II, Part I, 3472–73.

13. *Apol.* 1.26.3.

14. See John 7.27, 41, 52; 1.46.

15. *Apol.* 1.64.15.

16. Vincent, "La culte d'Hélène à Samarie," *Revue Biblique,* XLV (1936), 221–26; Quispel, *Gnosis als Weltreligion,* p. 62.

17. The coincidences between this account and what we have inferred from Justin increase the likelihood that Irenaeus is following Justin's lost treatise *Against All Heresies;* see also R. A. Lipsius, "Irenaeus," in *Dictionary of Christian Biography,* III (London, 1882), 260–61.

18. Cf. treatment of the prologue as a Gnostic "hymn" in Bultmann, *Das Evangelium des Johannes,* pp. 5–15.

19. John 1.6–8, 15.

20. See Vürtheim, *Stesichoros' Fragmente und Biographie,* frag. 11.

21. For this line, I follow Theodoret (cited by Harvey in Irenaeus *Adv. haer.* p. 192 n.3).

22. "And the angels" is perhaps an explanatory gloss.

23. See Alexander Polyhistor *De Iudaeis,* in Jacoby, *Die Fragmente der griechischen Historiker,* III A, 273 F 19, 102.

24. *Pan.* XXI.3.1–3.

25. *Ref.* VI.19.2–3.

26. Virgil *Aeneid* 6.518; Tryphiodorus *Halosis* 512f.; see also E. Norden, *Aeneis Buch VI* (2d ed; Leipzig, 1916), pp. 260–63.

27. Probably later Simonian clarification is provided in *Clementine Homilies* II.25.2: "Helen" was not really at Troy but was with the First God.

28. Plutarch *De Iside* 62; R. Marcus, "Note on an Aramaic Etymology in Plutarch," *American Journal of Philology,* LXIII (1942), 235.

29. Leisegang, "Sophia," in RE, III A, 1032–33.

30. *Hauptprobleme der Gnosis,* p. 81.

31. W. Drexler in W. H. Roscher, *Ausführliches Lexikon der griechischen und römischen Mythologie,* II (Leipsig, 1890–97), 500.

32. For the Sumerian myth, see S. N. Kramer in J .B. Pritchard, *Ancient Near Eastern Texts Relating to the Old Testament* (Princeton, 1950), pp. 52–57; also "Inanna's Descent to
the Nether World," *Journal of Cuneiform Studies*, IV (1950),
199–211; V (1951), 1–17.

33. For this, see E. A. Speiser in J. B. Pritchard, *Ancient
Near Eastern Texts*, pp. 106–9; see also Gressmann, *Altorien-
talische Texte zum Alten Testament*, pp. 206–10; Ganschi-
nietz, "Katabasis," RE, X, 2389–90; T. F. Glasson, "The Descent of Ishtar," *Congregational Quarterly*, XXXII (1954),
313–21.

34. Plutarch *De Iside* 62.

35. Diogenes Laertius, proem. 10.

36. Plutarch *De Iside* 27; Apuleius *Metamorphoses* 11.2, 4.

37. L. Mitteis and U. Wilcken, *Grundzüge und Chrestomathie der Papyruskunde*, I, Part 2 (Leipzig, 1912), 134–35
(No. 102).

38. *De Iside* 3.

39. *Leg.* 22.8.

40. It has been suggested that Sophia is the Jewish substitute
for Ishtar or Isis; see also G. Boström, *Proverbiastudien: Die
Weisheit und das fremde Weib in Spr. 1–9* (Lund, 1935); W. L.
Knox, "The Divine Wisdom," JTS, XXXVIII (1937), 230–37.

41. See C. Taylor, *Sayings of the Jewish Fathers* (Cambridge, 1897), pp. 58, 68; on the angel Israel, see also above,
pp. 18–19.

42. Further exegesis of Hosea occurs in the Baruch-book of
Justin (Hippolytus *Ref.* v.27.4) and the bride of Elohim is
called Eden and Israel (v.26.36). Sacred marriages criticized in
the second century: Didache 11.11; Irenaeus *Adv. haer.* 1.21.1
(Harvey p. 183); see also IV.20.12 (Harvey p. 223).

43. Harnack, Frag. 4; see also Origen *Princ.* III.5.6; *Commentary on John* XIII.59.

44. Ascension of Isaiah 10; Epistle of the Apostles 13; Ire-

naeus *Adv. haer.* 1.30.12 (Harvey p. 238), *Epideixis* 84; see also *Pistis Sophia* 7.

45. We need not identify the Holy Spirit either with Helen (R. P. Casey in F. J. F. Jackson and K. Lake, *The Beginnings of Christianity,* V [London, 1933], 158) or with Paul (H. A. Wolfson, *The Philosophy of the Church Fathers,* I [Cambridge, 1956], 516–17). The Holy Spirit could be in every Simonian. One can add that the sequence Son-Father occurs in Matt. 11.27.

46. See Schoeps, *Theologie und Geschichte des Judenchristentums,* pp. 37–61.

47. *Adv. haer.* 1.23.1 (Harvey p. 190).

48. Simon could have said, "It is no longer Christ who lives, but I who lived in him" (see Gal. 2.20). Simon was the Power of God and Helen the Wisdom of God (see 1 Cor. 1.24).

49. *Apol.* 1.26.4.

50. *Ref.* VI.9.4–18.7.

51. Origen *Commentary on John* XIII.27.

52. Photius *Bibl.* 230 (*Patrologia Graeca* 103, 1084D).

53. Silvestre de Sacy, *Chrestomathie arabe* (2d ed.; Paris, 1826), I, 335–37; Epiphanius *Pan.* XIII.

54. Leemans, Frag. 24.

55. On Simon and Dositheus, see Wilson, "Simon, Dositheus and the Dead Sea Scrolls," *Zeitschrift für Religions- und Geistesgeschichte,* IX (1957), 21–30.

56. Justin *Apol.* 1.26.4; Irenaeus *Adv. haer.* 1.23.5 (Harvey p. 195).

57. P. Carrington, *The Early Christian Church* (Cambridge, 1957), I, 315–16.

58. Origen *Contra Celsum* 1.57; see also VI.11.

59. See Wolfson, *Philo* (Cambridge, 1947), I, 127–31; II, 180–94.

60. See R. M. Grant, "The Decalogue in Early Christianity," HTR, XL (1947), 1–17.

61. Irenaeus *Adv. haer.* 1.31.1 (Harvey pp. 241–42). See also p. 60.

62. *Strom.* III.34.3–4.

63. Irenaeus *Adv. haer.* 1.25 (Harvey pp. 204–10); Clement *Strom.* III.27.3 (but the account of Carpocratian doctrine, *Strom.* III.5–9, is quite different from that given in Irenaeus; see especially *Strom.* III.9.3). For later developments see Schoeps, *Aus frühchristlicher Zeit,* pp. 260–65.

Notes to Chapter 4: THE UNKNOWN FATHER

1. Irenaeus *Adv. haer.* 1.26.1 (Harvey pp. 211–12); Eusebius *Ecclesiastical History* III.28.2, 5; Epiphanius *Pan.* XXVIII.6.1.

2. Gaius of Rome in Eusebius *Ecclesiastical History* III.28.2.

3. Irenaeus *Adv. haer.* 1.24.1–2 (Harvey pp. 196–98).

4. *Ibid.,* 1.30.6 (Harvey p. 232); Pseudo-Tertullian *Adv. omn. haer.* 2; Epiphanius *Pan.* XXXVII.4.1.

5. *Dialogus Adamantii* II.8.

6. *Right Ginza* V.1, p. 168.11.

7. *Left Ginza* II.1, p. 454.22. From Saturninus, S. A. Pallis, *Mandaean Studies* (London, 1926), pp. 186–87.

8. See also Ezek. 2.2.

9. See also Kroll, *De oraculis chaldaicis,* p. 67 n.2.

10. Epiphanius *Pan.* XLV.2.1.

11. Theophilus *Ad Autolycum* II.28.

12. "Die Erklärung des Namens Kajin in Gen. 4.1," *Zeitschrift für die alttestamentliche Wissenschaft,* XXXI (1911), 147–51.

13. *Ibid.,* XXXII (1912), 117–19; see also V. Aptowitzer, *Kain und Abel in der Agada* (Vienna, 1922), p. 117; L. Ginzberg, *The Legends of the Jews* (Philadelphia, 1939), V, 79.

14. *Dial.* 100.5.

15. Epiphanius *Pan.* XXXVII.4.4–5; XXXIX.2.1; XL.5.3 (see also

Puech in *Mélanges Cumont*, p. 937); Irenaeus *Adv. haer.* 1.31.1 (Harvey p. 241); Hippolytus *Ref.* v.27.22–23.

16. Apocryphon of John, p. 62. Bogomils and Cathari held a similar view; see, for example, Söderberg, *La religion des Cathares*, p. 99.

17. See Rev. 12.7; see also H. Windisch, *Der messianische Krieg und das Urchristentum* (Tübingen, 1907).

18. Clement *Strom.* III.63.2.

19. See 2 Esdras 3.5; see also "Chaldaeans" in Hippolytus *Ref.* v.7.6.

20. *Adv. haer.* 1.30.5 (Harvey p. 232).

21. "De oudste vorm van de gnostische mythe," *Nederlands Theologisch Tijdschrift*, VIII (1953), 20–25.

22. "Die Sektenschrift und die Iranische Religion," *Zeitschrift für Theologie und Kirche*, XLIX (1952), 315.

23. *He That Cometh* (New York, n.d.), p. 265.

24. Eisagoge 14, p. 170.36; 16, p. 172.4, 8, in Hermann, ed., *Platonis Dialogi.*

25. Leemans, Frag. 21; see also Beutler, "Numenios (9)," RE, Suppl. VII, 669–70.

26. Eusebius (*Praep. Evang.* VII.13.1; *Leg. alleg.* III.207.

27. See E. Percy, *Untersuchungen über den Ursprung de johanneischen Theologie* (Lund, 1939), p. 186 n.45.

28. Salmon, "Cainites," in *Dictionary of Christian Biography*, I (London, 1877), 382.

29. Origen *Contra Celsum* VI.27, 28; see also Chadwick, *Origen: Contra Celsum*, p. 344 n.2.

30. See Heinemann, "Antisemitismus," in RE, Suppl. V, 3–43; J. Leipoldt, "Antisemitismus," *Reallexikon für Antike und Christentum*, I, 469–76.

31. Certainly with the Naassenes we are well beyond Judaism; see J. Carcopino, *De Pythagore aux apôtres* (Paris, 1956), pp. 175–88.

Notes to Chapter 5: FROM MYTH TO PHILOSOPHY?

1. For the absence of philosophy in Gnosticism, see Wolfson, *The Philosophy of the Church Fathers,* I, 559–74.

2. J. P. Audet, "Affinités littéraires et doctrinales du 'Manuel de discipline,'" *Revue Biblique,* LX (1953), 41–82; on the importance of Greek elements, see R. Joly, *Revue des études anciennes,* V (1953), 394–406.

3. On 2 Clement, see H. Windisch, "Das Christentum des zweiten Clemensbriefes," in *Harnack-Ehrung* (Leipzig, 1921), pp. 119–34; Daniélou, *Théologie du Judéo-Christianisme,* pp. 326–37. One is tempted to ascribe 2 Clement to Hyginus, during whose episcopate neither Marcion nor Valentinus was excommunicated.

4. Irenaeus *Adv. haer.* 1.27.1; III.4.2 (Harvey pp. 214–15, 17). See also Harnack, *Marcion,* 31*–39*.

5. See also Meinhold, "Polykarpos (1)," in RE, XXI, 1685–89.

6. See "Notes on Gnosis," VC, XI (1957), pp. 145–47.

7. Harnack, *Marcion,* pp. 196–97 n.1.

8. *Pan.* XLI.1.1.

9. *Adv. haer.* 1.27.3 (Harvey pp. 218–19).

10. Harnack, *Marcion,* pp. 21*–22*.

11. For a modern attempt to solve the difficulty, see O. Cullmann, *The Early Church* (Philadelphia, 1956), pp. 59–75.

12. See Harnack, *Marcion,* p. 20*.

13. Van Unnik, "The 'Gospel of Truth' and the New Testament," in Cross, *The Jung Codex,* pp. 108–22.

14. John 16.12–14.

15. Tertullian *Adv. Valent.* 4.

16. Hippolytus *Ref.* VI.37.7–8; we should include with the Psalm the statement of Hippolytus in *Ref.* VI.42.2; see also "Notes on Gnosis," VC, XI, 149–51.

17. H. Gunkel *et al.*, "Die Oden Salomos," ZNW, XI (1910), 291–328; W. R. Newbold, "Bardaisan and the Odes of Solomon," *Journal of Biblical Literature*, XXX (1911), pp. 161–204; see also Stölten, "Gnostische Parallelen zu den Oden Salomos," ZNW, XIII (1912), 29–58. On the Gospel of Truth and the Odes see H.-M. Schenke, *Die Herkunft des sogenannten Evangelium Veritatis* (Göttingen, 1959), with the review by Daniélou in *Recherches de science religieuse*, XLVII (1959), 582–83.

18. Irenaeus *Adv. haer.* III.11.9 (Harvey p. 52).

19. "The Original Doctrine of Valentine," VC, I (1947), 43–73.

20. For silence at the beginning of things, see 2 Esdras 6.39.

21. Irenaeus *Adv. haer.* I.1.1–2, 2.2 (Harvey pp. 8–9, 15).

22. Harnack, *Marcion*, pp. 97–98.

23. *Excerpta ex Theodoto* 38.3.

24. Against this view, see Quispel, "La lettre de Ptolémée à Flora," VC, II (1948), 30–31.

25. *Vis.* I.3.4; *Mand.* I.1.

26. *Vis.* III.4.1–2.

27. Harnack, *Marcion*, p. 135.

28. Irenaeus *Adv. haer.* I.6.2–3 (Harvey pp. 55–56).

29. See Sagnard, *La gnose valentinienne*.

30. See A. Houssiau, *La christologie de saint Irénée* (Louvain, 1955).

31. See "Notes on Gnosis," VC, XI (1957), 147–48.

32. R. P. Casey, *The Excerpts from Theodotus by Clement of Alexandria* (London, 1935); Sagnard, *Clément d'Alexandrie: Extraits de Théodote.*

33. R. M. Grant, *The Letter and the Spirit* (London, 1957), p. 141.

34. A. Houssiau, *La christologie de saint Irénée*, pp. 236–47.

35. R. M. Grant, *The Letter and the Spirit*, pp. 62–73.

36. Pseudo-Tertullian *Adv. omn. haer.* 17; Tertullian *Adv. Valent.* 4.

37. Hippolytus *Ref.* VII.20.2–21.4; see also Hendrix, *De Alexandrijnsche Haeresiarch Basilides;* Waszink, "Basilides," in *Reallexikon für Antike und Christentum,* I, 1217–25.

38. See *Miracle and Natural Law in Graeco-Roman and Early Christian Thought* (Amsterdam, 1952), pp. 128–29.

39. "Negative Attributes in the Church Fathers and the Gnostic Basilides," HTR, L (1957), 145–56.

40. *Ibid.,* 153; Hippolytus *Ref.* VII.20.3.

41. Gospel of Truth, pp. 38.11, 37–39; 39.7.

42. *Ibid.,* p. 39.3–5.

43. See, for example, Kennedy, "Buddhist Gnosticism, the System of Basilides," *Journal of the Royal Asiatic Society,* 1902, 377–415.

44. Quispel, "L'homme gnostique (La doctrine de Basilide)," *Eranos Jahrbücher,* XVI (1948), 89–139.

45. Clement *Strom.* VII.106.4.

46. *Geschichte der griechischen Religion,* II, 586.

47. "Numenios (9)," in RE, Suppl. VII, 664–78.

48. See Puech, "Numénius d'Apamée," in *Mélanges Bidez,* pp. 745–78.

49. Nilsson, *Geschichte,* II, 460.

50. Kroll, *De oraculis chaldaicis,* pp. 15–18, 46–53.

51. *La révélation d'Hermès Trismégiste,* Vols. I–IV.

52. Van Moorsel, *The Mysteries of Hermes Trismegistus,* pp. 19–26. But some Gnostic systems have no savior; see also J. Duchesne-Guillemin, *Ormazd et Zoroastre* (Paris, 1953), p. 111.

53. Van Moorsel, *The Mysteries of Hermes Trismegistus,* p. 21; see also Gundel, "Poimandres," in RE, XXI, 1204–5.

54. *Contra Celsum* IV.51.

Notes to Chapter 6: GNOSTICISM AND EARLY CHRISTIANITY

1. "The 'Son' as Organ of Revelation," HTR, IX (1916), 382–415.

2. *Agnostos Theos* (Berlin, 1913), p. 307.

3. " 'Knowledge' in the Dead Sea Scrolls and Matthew 11.25–30," HTR, XLVI (1953), 113–39.

4. *The Parables of the Kingdom* (New York, 1935); see also J. Jeremias, *The Parables of Jesus* (New York, 1955), especially p. 159.

5. *Jesus and His Coming* (New York, 1957).

6. *Jesus: Gestalt und Geschichte* (Bern, 1957), pp. 117–20.

7. See, for example, Dodd, *New Testament Studies* (Manchester, 1953), pp. 67–128.

8. J. Lowe, "An Examination of Attempts to Detect Development in St. Paul's Theology," JTS, XLII (1941), 129–42.

9. H. Chadwick, " 'All Things to All Men' (I Cor. IX.22)," *New Testament Studies*, I (1954–55), 261–75; W. L. Knox, *St. Paul and the Church of the Gentiles* (Cambridge, 1939).

10. See also R. M. Grant, *The Letter and the Spirit* (London, 1957), p. 53.

11. W. Schmithals, *Die Gnosis in Korinth* (Göttingen, 1956); U. Wilckens, *Weisheit und Torheit* (Tübingen, 1959); both to be modified in relation to J. Weiss, *Das erste Korintherbrief* (Göttingen, 1910), and J. Dupont, *Gnosis* (Louvain, 1949).

12. *Stromateis* III. 29–33 (cf. I. 69. 6; VII. 41.1).

13. The angels of I Cor. 11.10 belong in an apocalyptic context; cf. H. J. Cadbury, "A Qumran Parallel to Paul," HTR, LI (1958), 1–2; J. A. Fitzmyer in *New Testament Studies*, IV (1957–58), 48–58.

14. G. Bornkamm, *Das Ende des Gesetzes* (Munich, 1952), pp. 139–56.

15. *Christus* und *die Kirche im Epheserbrief* (Tübingen, 1930).

16. See C. L. Mitton, *The Epistle to the Ephesians* (Oxford, 1951).

17. See F. C. Grant, *The Gospels* (New York, 1957), pp. 134–53.

18. Conzelmann, *Die Mitte der Zeit* (Tübingen, 1954), espe-

cially pp. 83–116; see also H. J. Cadbury, "Acts and Eschatology," in *The Background of the New Testament and Its Eschatology* (Cambridge, 1956), pp. 300–21.

19. On the meaning of ἐντός, see C. H. Roberts, "The Kingdom of Heaven (Lk. XVII.21)," HTR, XLI (1948), 1–8.

20. "The Fall of Jerusalem and the 'Abomination of Desolation,'" *Journal of Roman Studies*, XXXVII (1947), 47–54.

21. Acts 21.38–39.

22. Acts. 8.9–24.

23. C. H. Roberts, *An Unpublished Fragment of the Fourth Gospel* (Manchester, 1935).

24. C. Maurer, *Ignatius von Antiochien und das Johannesevangelium* (Zurich, 1949).

25. C. C. Tarelli, "Clement of Rome and the Fourth Gospel," JTS XLVIII (1947), 208–9; M. E. Boismard, "Clément de Rome et l'Évangile de Jean," *Revue Biblique*, LV (1948), 376–87.

26. P. Gardner-Smith, *St. John and the Synoptic Gospels;* E. R. Goodenough, "John a Primitive Gospel," *Journal of Biblical Literature*, LXIV (1945), 145–82.

27. K. G. Kuhn, "Die in Palästina gefundenen hebräischen Texte und das Neue Testament," *Zeitschrift für Theologie und Kirche*, XLVII (1950), 209–11; L. Mowry, "The Dead Sea Scrolls and the Background for the Gospel of John," *Biblical Archaeologist*, XVII (1954), 78–97; R. E. Brown, "The Qumran Scrolls and the Johannine Gospel and Epistles," *Catholic Biblical Quarterly*, XVII (1955), 403–19, 559–74 (reprinted in Stendahl, *The Scrolls and the New Testament*, pp. 183–207).

28. Dodd, *The Interpretation of the Fourth Gospel*, pp. 54–73; R. G. Bury, *The Fourth Gospel and the Logos-Doctrine* (Cambridge, 1940).

29. Dodd, *The Interpretation of the Fourth Gospel*, pp. 74–96; A. Schlatter, *Die Sprache und die Heimat des vierten Evangelisten* (Gütersloh, 1902); but for the language in which the Gospel was written see E. C. Colwell, *The Greek of the Fourth Gospel* (Chicago, 1931).

30. Dodd, *The Interpretation of the Fourth Gospel*, pp. 10–53, 97–114 (against Mandaean influence, pp. 115–30).

31. J. R. Harris, *The Origins of the Prologue to St. John's Gospel* (Cambridge, 1917).

32. C. F. Burney, "Christ as the APXH of Creation," JTS, XXVII (1925–26), 160–77.

33. See especially Odeberg, *The Fourth Gospel*, and Dodd, *The Interpretation of the Fourth Gospel.*

34. Retaining this sentence, against Bultmann, *Komm.*, p. 139 n.6.

35. For the tabernacling of God's Name among his people, see Jer. 7.12; Ezek. 43.7; Psalms of Solomon 7.6; Didache 10.2; Quispel, "Het Johannesevangelie en de Gnosis," *Nederlands Theologisch Tijdschrift*, XI (1956–57), 199.

36. Yet Clement argues that there is no difference between the Incarnation and the inspiration of the prophets (*Excerpta ex Theodoto* 19.2).

37. Moreover, God revealed "the end of the times" only to Abraham (2 Esdras 3.14), or also to Moses (14.5).

38. Retaining "water and," against Bultmann, *Komm.*, p. 98 n.2.

39. "Eine gnostische Formel im 4. Evangelium," ZNW, XVIII (1917), 49–63.

40. See also R. Beutler, *Philosophie und Apologie bei Minucius Felix* (Weidn, 1936), pp. 13–14.

41. Retaining these verses, against Bultmann, *Komm.*, p. 287 n.7.

42. See Bultmann, *Komm.*, p. 196, also p. 162.

43. *Ibid.*, pp. 174–77.

44. *Ibid.*, p. 98 n.2.

45. Maurer, *Ignatius von Antiochien und das Johannesevangelium.*

46. "The Heretics Combatted by Ignatius of Antioch," *Journal of Ecclesiastical History*, V (1954–55), 1–6.

47. Philad. 6.1.

48. *Ibid.*, 8.2.

49. Magn. 8.1.

50. *Ibid.,* 8.2; see also Philad. 9.2.

51. Smyrn. 2.1.

52. *Ibid.,* 5.2.

53. Trall. 5.2; see also Smyrn. 6.1 (Jude 8; 2 Pet. 2.10).

54. Smyrn. 7.1.

55. Magn. 10.1.

56. Smyrn. 6.2 (1 John 3.11; 4.11–12); Eph. 5.3 (1 John 2.19).

57. Even if this passage is ultimately based on Wisdom 18.14–15 (Cabaniss, "Wisdom 18:14f.: An Early Christmas Text," VC, X [1956], 97–102) it has undergone Gnosticizing.

58. Elsewhere (Smyrn. 1.1) Ignatius gives the explanation of Matt. 3.15.

59. *Religionsgeschichtliche Untersuchungen zu den Ignatius-briefen.*

60. *Gnostisches Gut und Gemeindetradition bei Ignatius von Antiochien.*

61. "The Silence of Bishops in Ignatius," HTR, XLIII (1950), 169–72.

62. "Wisdom 18:14f.: An Early Christmas Text," VC, X (1956), 97–102.

63. "L'étoile de Jacob et la mission chrétienne à Damas," VC, XI (1957), 121–38; *Théologie du Judéo-Christianisme,* pp. 237–47.

64. Clement *Excerpta ex Theodoto* 74–75.

Notes to Chapter 7: BEYOND JUDAISM AND CHRISTIANITY

1. Labib, *Coptic Gnostic Papyri in the Coptic Museum of Old Cairo,* I (Cairo, 1956), plates 80–99; J. Leipoldt, "Eine neues Evangelium? Das koptische Thomasevangelium über-setzt und besprochen," *Theologische Literaturzeitung,* LXXX-III (1958), 481–96; J. Doresse, *L'Évangile selon Thomas* (Paris, 1959); A. Guillaumont, H.-C. Puech, G. Quispel, N.

Till, Yassah 'Abd Al Masih, *The Gospel According to Thomas* (Leiden, 1959); R. M. Grant, D. N. Freedman, W. R. Schoedel, *The Secret Sayings of Jesus* (New York, 1960; enlarged German edition with Beitrag by J. B. Bauer, *Geheime Worte Jesu*, Frankfurt, 1960); R. McL. Wilson, *Studies in the Gospel of Thomas* (London, 1961).

2. See "Une collection de paroles de Jésus récemment retrouvée l'évangile selon Thomas," *Comptes rendus de l'Académie des Inscriptions et Belles-Lettres*, 1957, 146–67.

3. *Luc. hom.* 1, p. 5, 13 Bauer.

4. Other instances in B. Gärtner, *The Theology of the Gospel According to Thomas* (New York, 1961), pp. 113–14.

5. On these passages in the Didache see H. Köster, *Synoptische Überlieferung bei den Apostolischen Vätern* (*Texte und Untersuchungen*, LXV, Berlin, 1957), pp. 10–11; J.-P. Audet, *La Didaché* (Paris, 1958), pp. 112–13, 367–71, 441–42, 467–68.

6. See W. R. Schoedel, "Naassene Themes in the Coptic Gospel of Thomas," VC, XIV (1960), 225–34.

7. *Ibid.*, pp. 154–55.

8. Grant et al., *op. cit.*, p. 162; see also Saying 46/47.

9. Gärtner, *op. cit.*, pp. 173–74.

10. *Ibid.*, pp. 214–15.

11. Hippolytus *Ref.* V. 8. 44.

12. Gärtner, *op. cit.*, pp. 137–38.

13. Irenaeus *Adv. haer.* I. 24. 6 (Harvey p. 202); *Pistis Sophia*, c. 134; for its origin see page 102.

14. See the brilliant article of W. G. Kümmel, "Futuristische und präsentische Eschatologie im ältesten Christentum," *New Testament Studies*, V (1958–59), 113–26, translated in *Journal of Religion*, XLII (1963), 303–14.

15. Labib, *op. cit.*, plates 99–134; German translation and notes by H.-M. Schenke, "Das Evangelium nach Philippus," *Theologische Literaturzeitung*, LXXXIV (1959), 1–26; see also R. M. Grant, "Two Gnostic Gospels," *Journal of Biblical Literature*, LXXIX (1960), 1–11; English translation and commentary by R. McL. Wilson, *The Gospel of Philip* (London-New York, 1962); Coptic text and German translation by

W. Till, *Das Evangelium nach Philippos* (Berlin, 1963); see
H.-M. Schenke, "Die Arbeit am Philippos-Evangelium," *Theologische Literaturzeitung*, XC (1965), 321–32.
　16. *Pan.* XXVI. 13. 2.
　17. 6; see also 102 (somewhat conjecturally restored).
　18. See "The Mystery of Marriage in the Gospel of Philip,"
VC, XV (1961), 129–40.
　19. See *The Earliest Lives of Jesus* (London, 1961), pp.
80–81.
　20. The word for Spirit is thus feminine, as in the Gospel
of the Hebrews, and presumably comes from a Semitic language.
　21. *Adv. haer.* I. 24. 6 (Harvey pp. 202–3); see also "Gnostic Origins and the Basilidians of Irenaeus," VC, XIII (1959),
121–25. The texts are perhaps worth quoting. Irenaeus (Latin)
reads, *Judaeos quidem iam non esse dicunt, Christianos autem
nondum;* Epiphanius (*Pan.* XXIV. 5. 4) quotes this as Ἰουδαίους
μὲν ἑαυτοὺς μηκέτι εἶναι φάσκουσι, Χριστιανοὺς δὲ μηδέπω γεγενῆσθαι.
　22. See the article cited in note 18.
　23. Coptic published by W. Till, *Die gnostische Schriften
des koptischen Papyrus Berolinensis 8502 (Texte und Untersuchungen*, LX, Berlin, 1955), pp. 62–79; Greek fragment by
C. H. Roberts, *Catalogue of the Greek and Latin Papyri in
the John Rylands Library, Manchester*, III (1938), no. 463.
　24. Papyrus pp. 8, 14-9, 5.
　25. P. 9, 20.
　26. Pp. 10, 1-3; 18, 14; see also Philip 31, 32, 55.
　27. Hippolytus *Ref.* V. 7. 33; compare Thomas, Saying
113/111.

Notes to CONCLUSION

　1. Van Unnik, "The 'Gospel of Truth' and the New Testament," in Cross, *The Jung Codex*, pp. 101–3.

2. A. v. Harnack, *Lehrbuch der Dogmengeschichte* (Tübingen, 1931), I, 243-61.

3. Houssiau, *La christologie de saint Irénée* (Louvain, 1955); Kretschmar, *Studien zur frühchristlichen Trinitätstheologie* (Tübingen, 1956); Daniélou, *Théologie du Judéo-Christianisme* (Paris, 1958); Orbe, *Hacia la primera teología de la procesión del Verbo* (*Estudios Valentinianos*, I/1-2 = *Analecta Gregoriana*, XCIX-C, Rome, 1958). For a brief summary of Orbe's work see Daniélou in *Recherches de science religieuse*, XLVII (1959), 583-86.

4. *The Pattern of Christian Truth* (London, 1954), pp. 81-94.

5. Both Irenaeus (*Adv. haer.* v.34.1 [Harvey pp. 388-89]) and Theophilus (*Ad Autol.* 3.14) treat the "principalities and powers" of Rom. 13 as political rather than demonic.

6. On Montanism, gnosis, and persecutions, see Frend, "The Gnostic Sects and the Roman Empire," *Journal of Ecclesiastical History*, V (1953-54), 25-37.

BIBLIOGRAPHY

Albinus. In C. F. Hermann, ed., Platonis Dialogi, Vol. VI. Leipzig, 1880. Pages 147–89.

Alexander Polyhistor. In F. Jacoby, Die Fragmente der griechischen Historiker. Vol. III A. Leyden, 1940.

Apocryphon of John. In W. Till, Die gnostische Schriften des koptischen Papyrus Berolinensis 8502. Berlin, 1955. Also in P. Labib, Coptic Gnostic Papyri in the Coptic Museum at Old Cairo, Vol. I. Cairo, 1956.

Apokalypsen des Esra und des Baruch, Die. Ed. and tr. by B. Violet and H. Gressmann. Leipzig, 1924.

Apostolic Fathers. Patrum apostolicorum opera, ed. quinta minor, by O. von Gebhardt, A. Harnack, and T. Zahn. See also Didache; Hermas; Ignatius.

Athenagoras. In E. J. Goodspeed, Die ältesten Apologeten. Göttingen, 1914.

Barnabas. See Apostolic Fathers.

Baron, S. W. Social and Religious History of the Jews. 2d ed., rev. Vols. II (1952) and V (1957). New York, 1952, 1957.

Baruch, see Apokalypsen des Esra und des Baruch, Die.

Bauer, W. A Greek-English Lexicon of the New Testament and Other Early Christian Literature. Chicago, 1957.

Biblia hebraica. Ed. by R. Kittel. Stuttgart, 1937.

Bousset, W. Hauptprobleme der Gnosis. Göttingen, 1907.

Buch Henoch, Das. Ed. and tr. by J. Flemming and L. Rader-
macher. Leipzig, 1901.
Bultmann, R. Das Evangelium des Johannes. Göttingen, 1941.
Buttenwieser, M. "Apocalyptic Literature, Neo-Hebraic," in
Jewish Encyclopedia, I, 675–85. New York, 1901.
Canticles Rabbah. In H. Freedman and M. Simon, tr., Midrash
rabbah, Vol. IX. London, 1939.
Casey, R. P. The Excerpta ex Theodoto of Clement of Alex-
andria. London, 1935.
Chadwick, H., tr. Origen: Contra Celsum. Cambridge, 1953.
Chagigah. Hagigah, in I. Epstein, ed., The Babylonian Talmud.
Seder Mo'ed, Vol. VIII. London, 1938.
Clement (1 and 2), see Apostolic Fathers.
Clementine Homilies. Ed. by B. Rehm. Leipzig, 1953.
Clementine Recognitions. In J. P. Migne, ed., Patrologia
Graeca, I, 1201–1454.
Clement of Alexandria. Ed. by O. Stählin. 4 vols. Leipzig,
1905–36.
Cross, F. L., ed. and tr. The Jung Codex. London, 1955.
Daniélou, J. Théologie du Judéo-Christianisme. Paris, 1958.
Dead Sea Scriptures. Tr. by T. H. Gaster. New York, 1956.
Didache. In J. P. Audet, La Didaché. Paris, 1958. See also
Apostolic Fathers.
Dodd, C. H. The Interpretation of the Fourth Gospel. Cam-
bridge, 1953.
Doresse, J. Les livres secrets des gnostiques d'Egypte. Paris,
1958.
Enoch, see Buch Henoch, Das.
Epiphanius. Panarion. Ed. by K. Holl. 3 vols. Leipzig, 1915–
33.
Eusebius. Ecclesiastical History. Ed. by E. Schwartz. 2 vols.
Leipzig, 1905, 1909.
—— Praeparatio Evangelica. Ed. by K. Mras. 2 vols. Berlin,
1954, 1956.

Ezra, *see* Apokalypsen des Esra und des Baruch, Die.

Festugière, A. J. La révélation d'Hermès Trismégiste. 4 vols. Paris, 1944-54.

Gaster, T. H. The Dead Sea Scriptures. New York, 1956.

Genesis Rabbah. In H. Freedman and M. Simon, tr., Midrash rabbah, Vol. I. London, 1939.

Ginza. Der Schatz oder grosse Buch der Mandäer. Tr. and comm. by M. Lidzbarski. Göttingen, 1925.

Goodspeed, E. J. Die ältesten Apologeten. Göttingen, 1914.

Gospel of Truth. Evangelium Veritatis, ed. and tr. by M. Malinine, H. C. Puech, and G. Quispel. Zurich, 1956.

Harnack, A. von. Marcion: Das Evangelium vom fremden Gott. 2d ed. Leipzig, 1924.

Harvey, W. W., *see* Irenaeus.

Hendrix, P. De Alexandrijnsche Haeresiarch Basilides. Amsterdam, 1926.

Heracleon. In A. E. Brooke, ed., The Fragments of Heracleon. Cambridge, 1891.

Hermann, C. F., ed. Platonis Dialogi. 6 vols. Leipzig, 1874-80.

Hermas. Der Hirt des Hermas. ed. by M. Whittaker. Berlin, 1956. *See also* Apostolic Fathers.

Hermetica. Hermès Trismégiste. Ed. and tr. by A. D. Nock and A. J. Festugière. 4 vols. Paris, 1945-54.

Hippolytus. Refutatio. Ed. by P. Wendland. Leipzig, 1916.

Hyginus. Hygini Fabulae. Ed. by H. J. Rose. Leyden, n.d.

Ignatius. In J. B. Lightfoot, The Apostolic Fathers, Part II, Vol. II, Sect. 1. London, 1885. *See also* Apostolic Fathers.

Irenaeus. Adversus haereses. In W. W. Harvey, ed., Sancti Irenaei Episcopi Lugdunensis Libros Quinque Adversus Haereses. Cambridge, 1857.

—— Epideixis. Tr. by J. P. Smith, in St. Irenaeus, Proof of the Apostolic Preaching. Westminster, Md., 1952.

Jacoby, F. Die Fragmente der griechischen Historiker. Vol. III A. Leyden, 1940.

BIBLIOGRAPHY 229

Jonas, H. Gnosis und spätantiker Geist. 2 vols. Göttingen, 1934, 1954.

Josephus. Ed. By S. A. Naber. Leipzig, 6 vols. Leipzig, 1888–96.

Jubilees. The Book of Jubilees. Ed. and tr. by R. H. Charles. London, 1902.

Justin Martyr, Saint. Apologies. In E. J. Goodspeed, Die ältesten Apologeten, Göttingen, 1914.

—— Dialogue. In E. J. Goodspeed, Die ältesten Apologeten. Göttingen, 1914.

Kittel, G., ed. Theologisches Wörterbuch zum Neuen Testament, Vol. I. Stuttgart, 1932.

Kroll, W. De oraculis chaldaicis. Breslau, 1894.

Labib, P. Coptic Gnostic Papyri in the Coptic Museum at Old Cairo, Vol. I. Cairo, 1956.

Leemans, E. A. Studie over de Wijsgeer Numenius van Apamea met Uitgave der Fragmenten. Brussels, 1937.

Left Ginza, see Ginza.

Manual of Discipline. In The Dead Sea Scriptures. Tr. by T. H. Gaster. New York, 1956.

Marcion, see Harnack, A. von.

Nilsson, M. P. Geschichte der griechischen Religion, Vol. II. Munich, 1950.

Novum Testamentum Graece. Ed. by E. Nestle. Stuttgart, 1950.

Numenius, see Leemans, E. A.

Odeberg, H. The Fourth Gospel. Uppsala, 1929.

Odes of Solomon. Ed. and tr. by J. R. Harris. Cambridge, 1909; 2d ed., Manchester, 1921.

Oracula Chaldaica, see Kroll, W.

Oracula Sibyllina. Ed. by J. Geffcken, Leipzig, 1902.

Origen. Contra Celsum. Ed. by P. Koetschau. Leipzig, 1899. Also in H. Chadwick, tr. and comm., Origen: Contra Celsum. Cambridge, 1953.

—— Homilien zum Hexateuch. Ed. by W. A. Baehrens. 2
vols. Leipzig, 1920, 1921. Die Homilien zu Lukas. Ed. by
M. Rauer. Leipzig, 1930.

—— Der Johanneskommentar. Ed. by E. Preuschen. Leipzig,
1903.

—— Matthäuserklärung. Ed. by E. Klostermann. 2 vols.
Leipzig, 1933, 1935.

—— De principiis. Ed. by P. Koetschau. Leipzig, 1913.

Papias, see Apostolic Fathers.

Philo. Ed. by L. Cohn and P. Wendland. 7 vols. Berlin,
1896–1930.

Photius. Bibliotheca. In J. P. Migne, ed., Patrologia Graeca,
103.

Pistis Sophia. In C. Schmidt, Koptisch-gnostische Schriften,
Vol. I. Leipzig, 1905.

Polycarp. In J. B. Lightfoot, The Apostolic Fathers, Part II,
Vol. II, Sect. 2. London, 1885. See also Apostolic Fathers.

Pseudo-Tertullian, Adversus omnes haereses, see Tertullian.

Ptolemaeus, see Quispel, G.

Puech, H. C. "Fragments retrouvés de l'Apocalypse d'Al-
logène," in Mélanges Franz Cumont. Brussels, 1936. Pages
935–62.

—— "The Jung Codex and the Other Gnostic Documents
from Nag Hammadi," in F. L. Cross, ed. and tr., The Jung
Codex. London, 1955. Pages 11–34.

—— "Les nouveaux écrits gnostiques découverts en Haute
Egypte," in Coptic Studies in Honour of Walter Ewing
Crum. Boston, 1950. Pages 91–154.

—— "Numénius d'Apamée," in Mélanges Bidez. Brussels, 1934.
Pages 745–78.

Quispel, G. Gnosis als Weltreligion. Zurich, 1951.

—— ed. and tr. Ptolemée: Lettre à Flora. Paris, 1949.

Right Ginza, see Ginza.

Sagnard, F. M. Clément d'Alexandrie: Extraits de Théodote. Paris, 1948.
—— La gnose valentinienne et le témoignage de saint Irénée. Paris, 1947.
Schoeps, H. J. Aus frühchristlicher Zeit. Tübingen, 1950.
—— Urgemeinde—Judenchristentum—Gnosis. Tübingen, 1956.
Septuaginta. Ed. by A. Rahlfs. Stuttgart, 1935.
Söderberg, H. La religion des Cathares. Uppsala, 1949.
Solomon, see Odes of Solomon.
Stesichorus, see Vürtheim, J.
Tatian. In E. J. Goodspeed, Die ältesten Apologeten. Göttingen, 1914.
Tertullian. Ed. by F. Oehler. Leipzig, 1853.
Testaments of the Twelve Patriarchs. Ed. by R. H. Charles. Oxford, 1908.
Theodotus, see Casey, R. P.; also Sagnard, F. M., Clément d'Alexandrie: Extraits de Théodote.
Theophilus. Ad Autolycum. In J. C. T. Otto, Corpus apologetarum saeculi secundi, Vol. VIII. Jena, 1861.
Till, W. Die gnostischen Schriften des koptischen Papyrus Berolinensis 8502. Berlin, 1955.
Van Moorsel, G. The Mysteries of Hermes Trismegistus. Utrecht, 1955.
Van Unnik, W. C., "The 'Gospel of Truth' and the New Testament," in F. L. Cross, The Jung Codex. London, 1955. Pages 79–129.
Völker, W. Quellen zur Geschichte der christlichen Gnosis. Tübingen, 1932.
Vürtheim, J. Stesichoros' Fragmente und Biographie. Leyden, 1919.
War of the Sons of Light against the Sons of Darkness. In The Dead Sea Scriptures. Tr. by T. H. Gaster. New York, 1956.

Wolfson, H. A. The Philosophy of the Church Fathers, Vol. I. Cambridge, Mass., 1956.

Zadokite Document. In The Dead Sea Scriptures. Tr. by T. H. Gaster. New York, 1956.

INDEX

nine thought compared, 169-75;
and Ignatius of Antioch, 179-81;
struggle of early Church against,
197-200
Gnostics: as possessors of divine
spark, 107; as first Christian theologians, 197; as Christians, 204
note 44
God: in Gnostic systems, 15-23, 24;
Old Testament prophecies regarding action of, 27-30; Jewish
names for, 59; Supreme, of Gnostics, 97-98; Basilides on nature of,
143-45; Gospel of Truth on name
of, 145
Goodenough, E. R., cited, 102-3
Gospel of Truth, 5; on self-knowledge, 12; on ascent to heaven, 65;
Valentinus and, 128-34; on God's
name, 145; use of Gospel of John
in, 163
Grant, F. C., cited, 206 note 11
Greece, see Hellenism

Hadrian, 32
Haenchen, E., cited, 24
Haimatitoi, 7
Harnack, cited, 18, 125
Harris, Rendel, quoted, 132
Heaven: ascension to, 61-66; Jesus'
descent from, 66-69; see also
Aeons; Angels; Archons; Spirits
Hebrews (epistle), and Gospel of
Philip, 194
Hegesippus, cited, 14
Helen (of Troy): Simon Magus'
discovery of, 9; of Simonian doc-
trine, 74-81, 83-85; likened to lost
sheep, 86; in Eastern Simonian-
ism, 92
Hellenism: elements in Gnosticism,
2, 5, 26; Gnostic origins in, 13-15,
38, 46, 61, 113, 115; and Simonian-
ism, 78; as source of Simon's First
Thought, 80, 82, 83; philosophy

as basis of Basilides' system,
143-47; re soul, 202 note 16
Heracleon, 139
Heracles, 19, 22, 23, 24
Hermas, cited, 67, 122-23, 137, 144
Hermetica, 36, 166
Herod Antipas, 105
Hippolytus: as source, 3-4, 90; cited,
78-79, 132, 142-43, 147
Homer, 38, 79
Hosea, 85, 101, 212 note 42
Hyginus (bishop), 216 note 3
Hyginus (mythographer), 46
Hypostasis of the Archons, 6
Hystaspes, 31

Ignatius of Antioch, 94, 99, 163,
177-81, 197
Inanna, 81-82, 84
Iran: Gnostic origins in, 13, 15, 42,
46, 48-51, 52; dualism of, 56,
113-14; relation of Gnostic ideas
on ascent to heaven, 61
Irenaeus: as source, 3-5 passim; on
myth and Gnostic theology,
11-12; on Gnostic systems, 15, 16,
43, 46; on origin of heavenly
aeons, 54; on ascent to heaven,
64; on nature of Simon Magus,
70; on Simonianism, 75-77, 86-89;
on Saturninus, 108; and Apocryphon of John, 109; on Roman
heterodoxy before Marcion, 124;
on Marcion, 124, 126; on Gospel
of Truth, 134; on Ptolemaeus'
system, 139; effect of Valentinians on, 135, 141; on Basilides,
142-43
Isaiah (book of), cited, 60, 63, 64,
105, 106
Isaiah, Ascension of, 41
Ishtar, 81, 82
Isis, 81, 83-84

James, Protevangelium of, 104

note 40; *see also* Wisdom
Sophia of Jesus Christ, 5
Spirits, planetary, 46-51
Stauffer, E., cited, 154
Stesichorus, 77, 79
Syria, 125, 126, 135

Ten Commandments, 95
Tertullian, cited, 126, 132, 137-38; effect of Valentinians on, 141
Theodore bar Konai, 4
Theodotus, 139
Theophilus of Antioch: cited, 103; effect of Valentinians on, 141
Thessalonians, exegesis of, 155-56; 1 Thessalonians, cited, 66; 2 Thessalonians, cited, 36
Theudas, 29
Thomas, Gospel of, 6 182-90
Till, Walter, 5, 109
1 Timothy, cited, 161
Tiridates, 31
Titus (emperor), 31
Titus (epistle), 161
Tobit, cited, 46
Trajan, 32
Tryphiodorus, 79
Turner, H. E. W., cited, 197
Tyre, as source of Simonian First Thought, 81

Universe, origin of, 8; *see also* Creation; World

Valentinians definition of gnosis, 7-8; man's role according to, 9;
on aeons, 52-54; on ascent to heaven, 64; development of theology of, 134-42; and Gospel of Philip, 190
Valentinus, 5; on ascent to heaven, 65; and the Gospel of Truth, 128-34; and eschatological doctrines, 175
Van Moorsel, cited, 148
Van Unnik, cited, 129, 197
Vespasian, 30, 31
Virgil, 79

War Scroll, 43; *see also* Dead Sea Scrolls
Wetter, Gilles, cited, 171
Wisdom, 67, 153, 154
Wolfson, H. A., cited, 144
World: in Gnosticism, 8, 9, 10, 17; nature of, 20-21, 39-40, 53; between creation and redemption, 104-9; Saturninus' hostility toward, 107-8; *see also* Creation

Yahweh, 21; as Satan, 56-61; as Cain, 110; the name, 168-69

Zadokite Document, cited, 209 note 56
Zaehner, R., cited, 50
Zealots, 28-30 *passim*
Zephaniah, Apocalypse of, quoted, 18
Zeus, Simon worshiped as, 76
Zohar, 23
Zoroastrianism, 6, 52, 56
Zurvan, 49